T0368481

ENLIGHTEN
Your
PLATE

Plant-based & Gluten-free recipes from the
beloved Ezra's Enlightened Café

AUDREY BARRON

Balboa Press books may be ordered through booksellers or by contacting:

Balboa Press
A Division of Hay House
1663 Liberty Drive
Bloomington, IN 47403
www.balboapress.com
844-682-1282

Because of the dynamic nature of the Internet, any web addresses or links contained in this book may have changed since publication and may no longer be valid. The views expressed in this work are solely those of the author and do not necessarily reflect the views of the publisher, and the publisher hereby disclaims any responsibility for them.

Any people depicted in stock imagery provided by Getty Images are models, and such images are being used for illustrative purposes only.
Certain stock imagery © Getty Images.

Marci & Christy Photography and Kristy Murphy Photography

ISBN: 979-8-7652-3846-2 (sc)

Library of Congress Control Number: 2023901614

Print information available on the last page.

Balboa Press rev. date: 04/27/2023

TABLE OF CONTENTS

ACKNOWLEDGEMENTS

I have been blessed to have so very many people in my life who have supported me as I started my career as a Chef. I first must start with my husband, Sam. I remember the day I told him I wanted to leave my full-time successful career in Human Resources and travel to California to become a Raw Food Chef. He has trusted my instincts from the beginning. He knew that if I was going to make such a huge change in my life, I would put all I had into it, and I did. He became our resident handyman, helping to fix and repair things at the cafe and generally doing whatever I needed him to do. When we started the farm, he picked up our massive amount of compost every single week, taking it to the farm and dumping it himself. This was done every Sunday, rain, sleet or snow. He took care of our children when I needed to work on weekends early in the morning. He served as my therapist when times were hard. He gave support in so many ways I cannot possibly list them all here. Ezra's Cafe could have never existed without his support.

Living Light Culinary Institute, run by Cheri Soria at the time, was a HUGE inspiration for me in the endeavor to help people heal and thrive. I traveled there in 2009 for the Chef training program, nestled in the cost of beautiful Northern California, I learned from some truly talented Chefs and instructors. The school wove healing into everything we were taught, even when making beautiful cakes and desserts. This education fueled me to start teaching as soon as I arrived back in Indiana. That trip and those teachings changed my life forever.

My first teaching experiences were at health food stores, in homes, and at our local Whole Foods, which at the time put a focus on community engagement and brought in teachers like myself. My friend Sarah, who worked as the Marketing Director for our local Whole Foods at the time, was such a champion for me. She was so encouraging to a young person making her way in a new career as a chef and instructor. Sarah became a friend, and we eventually both became mothers on the journey.

Georgetown Market, run by my friend Rick, was and is a gem in our community. This health food store and grocery gave me a place to teach. I still remember teaching, very pregnant, and telling my students about this cafe I was soon going to open. Rick became a friend and champion for me and I am incredibly grateful for the wisdom he shared and the support he gave to me.

Good Earth, my neighborhood health food store, brought me in to teach classes before the cafe opened and supported me from the beginning. They became one of our trusty suppliers that we relied on throughout the lifetime of the cafe, helping us in times when supply of certain items was hard to find.

We held two crowdfunding campaigns for Ezra's Cafe. We had so many folks generously give to the cause, which not only gave us financial support but gave me the resolve to keep going when we were running into hurdle after hurdle to get the cafe open.

In getting our doors open, I remember my cousin, Kyle, helping to get our signs made and my father painstakingly making our first bar in his shop and installing it for us. My father also helped with other carpentry projects we needed. He loved to come in and razzle my employees and make them laugh. He was so proud of me. He passed in early 2020 right before the pandemic hit. My mother helped with the children when both my husband and I had to work, especially on holidays, which was always so helpful. It truly does take a village.

I also want to acknowledge my dear friend, Wendell Fowler, who supported me from the day I told him I was thinking of opening the cafe. With decades of experience in the food industry, he was often a listening ear when I needed to vent or talk through a challenge. Everyone needs a friend like Wendell. Love you my friend.

We had many employees over the years. It was their hands that made the food day in and day out for our customers. It was our employees who carried out the daily, and hourly tasks that kept the cafe going for those 7.5 years.

Many of our vendors became friends and community contacts who we cared about. So many of them worked with us and made sure we had the supply we needed as soon as we needed it.

In the making of this book, I've had the help of two amazing ladies, Leigh and Nora, who have helped edit and proofread.

Lastly, I want to acknowledge our thousands of customers. It was for you that we existed, and it was you who came through our doors every single week for 7.5 years to support us and show us that we mattered in your lives. Over the years, some of you have become true friends. You've shown your support through your words, your hugs, your letters, your tips to our staff, and through simply being a patron. Some of you were passing through and some were regulars who became known by our staff. I remember on that last day we were open, a woman came up to me and told me she had flown in from Texas for our last day. We embraced with tears in our eyes. I don't know your name, but that is something I will never forget. Thank you. Thank you for being our customers. Thank you for brightening our lives. You will forever be part of Ezra's Enlightened Cafe's legacy.

DEDICATION

For Ezra and Elliana. You both inspire me every single day to live life to the fullest.

You can do anything you put your mind to. Don't ever forget that.

OUR STORY

For a short while, 7.5 years, there was a little café. Nestled in an eclectic hippie neighborhood in Indianapolis called Broad Ripple, this space was an oasis for folks who valued food without pesticides and food that lifted them up. Ezra's Café was Indiana's first 100% gluten-free and NON-GMO café. Also completely plant-based, Ezra's was unique and for many, an oasis of healing food, education and community.

I opened Ezra's Café not long after giving birth to my first child, Ezra. Having been a plant-based Chef for years and teaching classes all over the city and beyond, I knew people were hungry for a place to take their family, knowing the food was safe. The two most common questions from my students were, "Where do you eat out in this town?" and "When are you opening a cafe?".

At the time, in addition to teaching cooking classes and personal Cheffing, I had a massage practice next door to the space that became Ezra's Cafe'. I would joke with my friends and co-workers, Vicki and Wendy, about opening a little café in the small garage attached to the house. Many of the small businesses in our neighborhood were in previous early homes (part of the charm). One day, something told me to ask the landlord for the key to the garage and so I did. I walked into that space to see an old armchair in the corner and random boards in another. A forgotten garage that seemed to be asking for a new story. I sat on the floor in silence and closed my eyes. I felt an energy there. I felt the people who would walk through the doors. I could feel the café already forming, almost like it already had its own life. I walked out of that garage with what I can only describe as a current of energy.

That current took me through a year and a half of planning, hours in the city- county building working on zoning, countless sleepless nights planning and wondering how I was going to do this. I did this all with my baby boy by my side, sleepless nights as a nursing mama, and my husband cheering me on. In the early stages, we rolled out a Kickstarter crowdfunding campaign and raised more than what we asked for. I knew then that this wild cafe dream would work. We had the support and energy of the community behind us. Little by little, we transformed that two-car garage into a bustling love-filled, energy-filled café. In our first week, we had a line out the door every day. And so it began. We served customers 6 days a week for those seven plus years.

Along the way, our family expanded and Ezra became a big brother to Elliana. Our family was growing and we watched so many of our customers grow their families as well. Over the years we said goodbye to some beloved customers who passed, we celebrated marriages, graduations and new babies. We watched life happen before our eyes. We were written up in multiple articles, won multiple awards in our state, and nationally. We even ended up on the Cooking Channel in 2016. The café became her own entity and we were along for the ride.

About a year after opening Ezra's Café, we purchased six acres of land, 10 minutes away and began a small urban farm to grow carrots, beets, kale, collards, herbs, tomatoes, peppers and more for our café menu. Our farm became a restorative part of the ecosystem of Ezra's Café. We held volunteer days each month; Spring through Fall for six years. This experience of growing our own food, and that food finding its way into our heartfelt dishes, was truly a beautiful experience. We learned what it takes to grow food using permaculture practices, and without chemicals. It was so very rewarding, challenging, and everything in between. This experience deepened our appreciation for our local farmers and for what it takes to put food on the plate.

When we opened, we were considered 100% raw – nothing cooked over 118°. We offered juices, smoothies, herbal tonics, desserts, one soup and the Buddha Bowl salad. Following our customer's lead, we quickly added hot soups and cooked foods to the menu. Our menu grew, along with the café over the years and expanded to smoothie bowls, lunch bowls, many more desserts, and specialty entrees. Our focus was always amazingly delicious food that was well balanced and vibrating with life. We wanted our customers to leave with more than a full belly. Our goal was for folks to leave feeling better than when they arrived.

We were unique in not only our menu, but our vision and the way we chose to operate our business. From the first day to our last, we held a team meeting in the morning before customers arrived. At the end of the meeting, we lit a candle, dedicated to someone who needed love, prayers or positive energy. Often, it was a customer we knew going through a hard time. Sometimes it was a family member of the team and sometimes a family or person in the news. This ritual carried us through those seven plus years with a positive heart-opening thread to start the day.

We had one rule for the team, which was kindness to each other and the customers at all times. While there are always hiccups in the road, we did our best to keep this rule true and it was a constant place to start each day and goal to achieve.

In the first few years, we had a jar at the register with inspirational quotes to pull out. Our customers loved grabbing one with their order. We also had a beautiful chalk tree painted on the wall, big enough to fill with an inspirational quote.

Sketch books and colored pencils were provided at the bar, for folks to draw and be creative.

What we experienced from these unique and heartfelt threads woven into the café, was love and dedication from our customers that we could have only dreamt. They appreciated the energy that we put into our offerings and we, in turn, received so much appreciation and love. This love from our customers carried us through some hard times, especially during the pandemic of 2020.

We had fun with our menu as it grew. Our customers gave feedback on what they enjoyed and wanted more of and even helped us name some menu items! They taste tested for us and we slowly built a menu that was deeply beloved.

This is what you'll find here in this recipe book. Time-tested, customer-loved recipes that nourished and delighted thousands of humans over the span of our time serving the community. It's rare to find a recipe book where the recipes have been this well-loved before the book is even written.

While Ezra's Enlightened Café has had her time in the sun, the memories remain. You'll find pictures of not only our food but our beautiful space here in this book. If you ever ventured to Ezra's Café, perhaps these photos will spark a happy memory for you. If you never had the opportunity to be in our space, you'll get a peek into how our small space felt.

Lastly, thank you for making these recipes in your home and carrying on the legacy of Ezra's Café. Many of these recipes I created in my small home kitchen with baby Ezra snuggled in his carrier on my chest, with only that electric energy of the café in my heart. And now it's time to set them free.

In Deep Gratitude,
Audrey

WHY NON-GMO?

We opened a plant-based, gluten-free eatery in a state where you can find fast food, fried chicken and burger joints in every town. To say we were unique is an understatement. Beyond that, we were dedicated to being NON-GMO and serving an almost 100% organic menu. This meant our cost to operate was much higher than the neighboring eatery. Our dedication to high quality food also meant sourcing could be hard at times.

One might wonder why we would take the road less traveled, which also meant it took more work for less money.

First let's talk about GMO's for a moment. A GMO, or genetically modified organism, is a plant, animal, microorganism or other organism whose genetic makeup has been modified in a laboratory using genetic engineering or transgenic technology. This creates combinations of plant, animal, bacterial and virus genes that do not occur in nature or through traditional crossbreeding methods.

This genetic modification is done to create a desired effect for the company growing the food. For instance, certain soy and corn crops are genetically modified to withstand high amounts of Glyphosate (also known as Roundup), which is a highly toxic herbicide linked to cancer and many other health issues. Each season, the farmers saturate the plants in this chemical to keep the weeds down, creating a better yield. While good for business, this means the land is being bathed in this chemical. The use of these herbicides has led to a decline in native plants, native insects and a surge in weeds resistant to the chemicals which require even more spray. It's a cycle taking us into a scary place in terms of toxicity to the soil and the planet at large.

In 1994, the first genetically modified household item hit grocery stores - the slow ripening tomato. I remember my parents saying tomatoes from the grocery store are never as good as from the home garden, and I agreed. Perhaps this was one of the reasons why. No longer was the flavor and nutrient content important - our food system was shifting to more of a profit-driven business. How to sell as much product as possible and make money for the high up executives was the priority over the health of the citizens purchasing the food.

Since that time, we have seen over and over again how processed food (much of it containing GMO soy, wheat and canola) is directly linked to the rise in obesity, heart disease, cancers, a decline in fertility, mental health and the list goes on.

So where does veganism intersect with the GMO issue? I often pondered this as a plant-based Chef and restaurant owner. If a person was vegan, primarily to not cause harm to animals, I wondered how so many vegan folks were totally okay with canola oil and the highly sprayed and genetically modified wheat products.

I realized there was a disconnect.

Many people simply have not spent time on the land growing food, to understand the impact a GMO crop has on not only the soil but the inhabitants of the land.

The crops planted with this GMO seed are known as mono-crops, meaning for acres and acres, only one crop is planted. In Indiana where I grew up, we would drive for miles in the countryside, only seeing miles and miles of corn fields. While it could be a beautiful site, this lack of diversity is detrimental to our wildlife and our soil year after year. The deer, coyotes, rabbits, frogs, groundhogs….thousands of animals, and insects that once thrived in the diversity of the forest or plains on these lands are being displaced and killed with each season. Not only are they dying from the toxic spray but the absolute lack of diversity of life. The soil on these monocrop farms are being depleted by year after year of tilling and spraying. When you see these farmlands in the fall and winter after the crops have been harvested, you see lifeless soil, dusty and bleached of its rich natural color.

All of this to say, consuming GMO corn, soy and canola is contributing directly to the depletion of our soil and the displacement and die-off of animal and insect species who once relied on those lands. This includes our precious bees who die by the millions each year from chemical spraying.

We, as a restaurant serving our community, did not want to contribute to this type of massive destruction to the planet and animals. Nor did we want to serve sprayed or genetically modified organisms to our customers.

Growing food all of my life and now on a bigger scale at our farm, I have seen there truly is no way to create a garden without displacing animals and insects. When we clear land in any form, there is death.

But when we garden and farm small and without chemicals, we give the land and the animals a chance to be part of the story. And we can even find ways to work with the local wildlife when we keep our food systems small and intentional.

This leads me into another hot topic on the vegan world, which is the use of honey. We used raw local honey from a long-time beekeeper at the restaurant from day one. As someone who works with natural medicines, I have used honey for decades to feed my family and in use as a medicine. Honey has been used by humans for thousands of years. It is only, again, in the last few decades that corn syrups and beet sugars were introduced to our collective processed food menu. Both being GMO and both being detrimental to human health, I find honey to be a much better option. Not only as a replacement to the lesser sugars but offering nutrients that actually nourish our cells and support our ultimate well-being.

Supporting our local beekeepers means the population of our honey bees are being managed and cared for, in a sea of GMO crops all around us. While I appreciate and understand the stance so many vegan folks take on honey, I find the conversation often lacks the full spectrum of what is happening in our food system. Ezra's Cafe' lovingly used our local honey and bee pollen for 7.5 years and we were proud to do so.

So there you have it. We chose to serve what we felt was best for not only our customers, but for the Earth herself. It is not enough to give ourselves a label such as "vegan" and be done with the conversation. We must look deeper at the farming practices and the reality of what it takes to put the food on our plate.

When we enlighten our plate, we enlighten our lives. When we enlighten our lives, we enlighten the planet.

And so it is.

INGREDIENT GUIDE

Ezra's Café menu was founded on quality, always and forever, quality. When we start with food that has been treated without chemicals and poisons, we are not only giving ourselves a gift, we are supporting a way of life for the farms, the farm workers and the planet to exist in a truly healthier way. From the first day we opened, our menu was fully NON-GMO and as organic as we could be – 90-99% at any given time. Exceptions would be things like avocados, which were on the "clean 15 list". We NEVER used canola oil, only organic olive and coconut oil.

We knew that sourcing everything organic, from our nuts and seeds to our oils and spices, would mean a much smaller profit margin for our café. Even with higher prices than eateries in our area who were serving mostly conventional/sprayed food, we still had a very small margin. We knew this and did it anyway, because Ezra's Café was created to be an oasis of nourishment and healing energy above anything else. It was about providing our community with the gift of food made with so much intention and love that we became a beacon. And that we did. Folks drove hours to eat with us every week, many from the neighboring states. And that was not taken for granted. When you build a foundation that is strong with clear intention, the energy of abundance will flow your way.

Okay so let's talk a bit more about chemicals. The Latin definition of "cide" is "killer" or "act of killing". So, when we see herb*icide*, fung*icide*, pest*icide*, etc., this tells you what that chemical is doing. Killing life.

These killer chemicals not only harm us, they are killing our precious topsoil and killing our pollinators by the millions every year. We cannot survive life as we know it without our topsoil and pollinators. Sadly, every year we are losing more of both due to mono GMO farming.

All this to say, organic ingredients are worth the extra money it costs. Staying away from these "killer" chemicals is, in my opinion, a great idea. Think of it as a direct and immediate investment in your health for today and for your future. And bonus – you are voting with your dollar in support of farming and food without chemicals.

When you can, I highly recommend supporting your local no-spray farmers. We make it a point to head to the farmers market as often as we can as a family, to support the growers providing food without chemicals. The connection to purchasing your food directly from the humans who grow it, is a special thing. This is how community is woven.

Beyond the farmers market, growing your own veggies and herbs connects you with your food and gives the comfort of knowing exactly how and where it was grown. I truly believe, when we procure as much of our food outside the parameters of the grocery store as possible, we are actively investing in our health and the future of our planet.

Now let's take a look at some of the special and less common ingredients you'll find in this book.

Almond pulp is the pulp that remains after making your almond mylk. Once you blend your almonds with water and strain, you will have a moist fibrous pulp that is essentially the skin and fiber of the almonds, with much of the fat removed. This pulp can be frozen and used later to make things like cookies, breads, bagels and crackers.

Bee pollen is flower pollen packed by worker honeybees, and used as the primary food source for the hive. It consists of simple sugars, proteins, minerals and vitamins, fatty acids, and a small percentage of other components. Humans have been consuming this highly nutrient-dense food for thousands of years. Bee pollen is a beautiful addition to your diet to bring in those important nutrients to your body. You'll find that we use bee pollen to top some of our smoothie bowls and even on or in some desserts.

Cacao butter is an edible fat that is extracted from the whole cacao beans. We used this beautiful fat to create firm chocolate layers, firm up a cake filling or to make chocolates.

Cacao nibs are crushed pieces of the cacao beans. We use these to sprinkle into or over a dessert, or in a smoothie to add chocolate flavor and crunch. The beans are also high in minerals and nutrients such as magnesium.

Cacao powder is the cacao bean processed at low temperatures and then milled into a powder. Cacao powder is quite bitter, but retains more of the bean's original nutritional value. Not to be confused with cocoa powder, which goes through higher temperatures and sometimes chemical processing. The cacao powder is processed in a way that preserves more of the nutrients and mineral content of the cacao bean.

CBD oil – Cannabidiol is a phytocannabinoid discovered in 1940 and one of 113 identified cannabinoids in cannabis plants. Over the past decade, CBD has been legalized for use in the United States and became popular as a treatment for epileptic seizures. Now, CBD is widely sold as a treatment for stress, anxiety and physical pain. We brought CBD into the café menu for select items. Customers would add it to smoothies and herbal tonics as well. We used only fully organic and high quality full-spectrum CBD oil.

Coconut butter is made by grinding the meat of a coconut into a butter-like consistency. We used this in select dessert recipes to help firm up a chocolate or cake filling.

Coconut flour is a gluten-free flour alternative made by grinding dried coconut into a powder. You can add this to a crust to help make it even and firm.

Coconut sugar is an all-natural sweetener derived from the sap of coconut palm flowers. It tastes and looks a lot like brown sugar and can be used in the same ways.

Dandy Blend is an instant coffee substitute made of only four ingredients: roasted barley extracts, roasted rye extracts, roasted dandelion root extracts, and roasted chicory root extracts. Due to the kind of water extraction processing the ingredients go through, the gluten is removed. This is an excellent addition to herbal lattes and to use in chocolate desserts.

Dried dates – Just like it sounds, these are a dried fruit that many call nature's candy. Dried dates are incredibly sweet and rich, making them amazing in desserts, especially raw crusts, accompanied by nuts.

Dulse flakes - Dulse is a red seaweed harvested in the cool waters and is an excellent source of phytochemicals and minerals, and a superior source of iodine.

E3Live and BrainON are superfood blends that include the E3Live brand's signature AFA and also a PEA extract for focus and mood balance. We used this in some smoothies and to color our mint cheesecake.

Goji Berries, also known as wolfberries, are a reddish-orange berry with a sweet and sour flavor that are native to Asia. Goji berries have the highest concentrations of melatonin and the third-highest antioxidant capacity of any common dried fruit – five times more than raisins and second only to dried pomegranate seeds and barberries. Our favorite goji berries can be found at Dragon Herbs. https://www.dragonherbs.com/

Hemp seeds (or Hemp hearts) are the seeds of the hemp plant. Hemp hearts are seeds that have had the shell removed. Hemp seeds are high in soluble and insoluble fiber as well as Omega 3's. They can be sprinkled over salads or any dish you desire. They can also be made into hemp mylk or added to smoothies.

Honey (raw local) is the result of a colony of bees working together to collect flower nectar and transform it into a high-energy source for the hive. Humans have been using honey for thousands of years to nourish, sweeten dishes and as medicine. We loved supporting our local beekeepers and bees to provide high quality honey to our customers.

Maple syrup is the boiled down sap of the maple tree that flows in late winter. It is richly sweet and very high in minerals such as iron, calcium and potassium. The maple syrup we used at Ezra's was supplied locally by small family syrup businesses. We loved using maple syrup to sweeten granolas and cakes.

Mesquite powder comes from a tree pod native to the desert climates of Peru, Colombia and Ecuador. It is considered a superfood high in minerals and nutrients known to help prevent diabetes, degenerative diseases and inflammation. Mesquite has a naturally sweet molasses flavor.

Miso is a fermented food most commonly made using soybeans. It can also be made with some combination of other beans, rice, or barley. Its texture is usually paste-like and relatively thick, similar to that of peanut butter. The base of miso is combined with salt and a fungus culture called koji kin, which is also used to make sake and soy sauce. We used chickpea miso in dressings and sauces to create a bold and rich flavor.

Nutritional yeast is an inactivated form of yeast commonly used to leaven bread. Nutritional yeast looks like red pepper flakes, only yellow, or powdered Parmesan cheese, with which it shares a deceptively similar flavor, despite being non-dairy. We used it to flavor sauces, dressings, cheezes and sometimes soups.

Shredded coconut consists of thin pieces of coconut, usually sold in dried form, and can be used in pie or cake crusts or to make your own coconut mylk.

Spirulina is a blue-green algae that is known to contain powerful anti-inflammatory components including chlorophyll, omega-3 fatty acids, and phycocyanin, an antioxidant. We used Spirulina in some smoothies as well as desserts to add a bright green color.

Stevia is a bushy shrub, best known as a natural sweetener. Stevia contains chemicals that are 200-300 times sweeter than sucrose sugar. This sweetening plant has become popular as a low glycemic way of sweetening a drink or dish.

Sun Warrior protein powder is a specific brand of protein powder we used at the café. You can find their products at https://sunwarrior.com.

Tahini is a paste made of sesame seeds, typically used in Middle Eastern and Mediterranean dishes. The thick paste is used to make hummus but can be used to make all types of sauces. Tahini is a high source of plant-based calcium.

Tamari is a Japanese sauce made from fermented soybeans. It has a thicker consistency and a more balanced flavor than Chinese soy sauce, making it a good choice for a dipping sauce. We always used the low sodium, gluten-free organic options.

EQUIPMENT GUIDE

Blenders – We used only Vita-Mix blenders at Ezra's. They are very high quality and high speed, making it easy and quick to blend a cake filling, dressing, sauce or smoothie. You are left with a very professional quality product.

https://www.vitamix-blenders.com/

Dehydrators – We used Excalibur dehydrators at Ezra's. They have models with temperature controls as well as timers. I recommend getting the 9-tray, as the smaller dehydrators aren't big enough for anyone wanting to make larger quantities. You can also use these to dry herbs if you have an herb garden. You will see we use the term "Teflex sheets" to reference the smooth sheets that come with your dehydrator. Excalibur has now coined the term Paraflexx sheets. They are the same thing.

https://excaliburdehydrator.com/

Juicers – There are so many juicer options out there. As a slow juicer that retains the nutrients very well, I found the Omega masticating juicer to be high quality and great for the Ginger Turmeric Immune Boost. I also think the Champion juicer is an easy-to-use slow juicer with a reputation for lasting decades.

For a faster juicer or one that can take more produce at a time, I like the Breville juicers.

https://omegajuicers.com/
https://championjuicer.com/
https://www.breville.com/

Nut mylk bags – You can definitely find nut mylk bags marketed by companies and they are often anywhere from $10-$20. For years, I have recommended to my students that you can find the same type of bags in the hardware store paint aisle, sold as paint-straining bags. They are quite affordable and come in 1 gallon and 5 gallon sizes. Sold in packs, they end up being $1 or so a bag.

Silicone cupcake molds – You can easily find these online or at your local kitchen supply store. They work perfectly for making our Carrot Spice Muffins, because they fit well in the dehydrator and make it easy to retrieve the muffins by peeling back the silicone.

Springform pans – These pans are necessary for the raw vegan cakes in this book. The springform option gives you the ability to easily take the cake out of the form without damaging the cake or needing to dig it out of a baking pan. You can find them in various sizes. For the cakes in this book, you can use either an 8 or 9 inch pan.

Tart pans – We use these for the brownies, lemon squares and more. You want the tart pans that have the removable bottom, to easily pop the dessert out, similar to the springform pan. This ensures your dessert is easy to remove from the pan and looks beautiful.

EZRA'S ORGANIC FARM

In 2015, my Husband, Sam and I made a huge life decision. We purchased six acres of land, minutes from the café with the vision of growing food for the cafe' and to bring the community together. This wild land had been sitting untouched for over 20 years. Full of invasive honeysuckle and vines choking out the trees, we had a lot of work ahead of us. But we were so very up for the challenge. Our vision was to start a small farm to grow food for Ezra's and to create a community gathering space. And we made it happen. At the time, we called her Ezra's Organic Farm.

In 2016, we planted our first crops and off we went. It was the most satisfying experience to harvest the kale and bring it into the kitchen to then watch as it landed on customer's plates.

A huge part of Ezra's Café was our commitment to leaving as little of a footprint as possible. We started out paying to have our food scraps picked up each week by a local compost company. And once we started the farm, we had a place to bring our scraps and start our own compost pile. For those 6 years, my husband Sam picked up our 5-6 industrial trash cans worth of scraps with our small trailer and dumped them by hand. We did the math and we were composting anywhere from 5,000 to 6,500 gallons of food scraps per year. In fact, for the life of Ezra's Café, we only used a 30 gallon trash can per week for actual trash. The rest went to compost and recycling.

Let's talk cardboard for a minute. At Ezra's Organic Farm, we used the permaculture practice of sheet mulching, which is the use of brown cardboard and mulch to keep the weeds down. This practice is amazing at not only cleaning up an area riddled with weeds, but to nourish the soil. The cardboard breaks down under the inches of mulch in about 6 months, and begins to feed the microbes in the soil. It actually helps to build soil over time. And in this process, we were using a lot of the cardboard that would have gone to recycling.

Each month, Spring through Fall, we offered volunteer days and wow did we meet some amazing folks. The community came out each month to help us tend to this wild land and those were some of our favorite times. We still hold these volunteer days even after the café closed. What we have seen in these years of holding volunteer days is that folks are hungry to get their hands in the dirt. Hungry to learn and reconnect to the old ways of growing our own food.

Over time, we grew more and more medicinal herbs at our farm. Being an Herbalist, I loved the idea of also selling some of our own tea blends, tinctures and oils and thus we did.

LOOKING FORWARD AT WILD MOON ACRES

Wild Moon Acres is our new name as we shift our focus to growing medicinal herbs, offering community workshops, and generally continuing our vision of being of service.

We grow medicinal herbs, elderberry trees and create beautiful herbal medicines and offerings from the plants we grow and forage.

Along with getting herbs and medicines into the hands of humans, we are also offering workshops and retreats centered around home herbalism, foraging and living in tune with nature.

To see what we are currently up to, you can find us at www.wildmoonacres.love and @wild.moon.acres on Instagram.

If you want to connect directly with me and the programs I offer, including my online home herbalism program, check out www.gaiachef.com .

A FEW THINGS TO KNOW BEFORE DIVING INTO THE RECIPES

Every recipe in this book was served to customers at Ezra's Cafe'. Some were on our permanent menu and some, only served for a short time. Everything in this book is dairy-free and gluten-free.

You will see we use the spelling "mylk" instead of milk. This is in respect for the milk that comes from our precious animals. The "mylk" we make are from plants - a beautiful option for those who cannot or do not want to consume dairy.

We use the spelling "cheeze" in place of cheese. This again, is in respect for the cheese made from animal products by our ancestors for thousands of years. The "cheeze" we make is from nuts - a beautiful option for those who cannot or do not want to consume cheese from dairy.

CHAPTER

1

JUICES

Fresh organic juices were a staple at Ezra's Café from day one. Over the years, we honed our recipes and expanded our juice menu. We created our juices to be as balanced as possible with sweet and savory flavors, while also bringing in a wide variety of nutrients. Fresh juices provide a straight shot of vitamins and nutrients with little to no fiber. They can be used as a way to gently flush the body of built up toxins and added weight, or simply as a vitamin-rich shot of goodness.

We never bottled our juices, as once a veggie or fruit is juiced, it's best consumed within 24 hours. Honestly it's best within the hour, if possible.

We had fun with our juice names as you'll see. We often created the names of juices and menu items as a team, which was super fun and gave our team a bit of ownership in our menu.

Making these juices at home:

My favorite home juicer at the time of writing this book is the Omega slow masticating juicer, which you can read more about in the equipment section at the beginning of this book. It provides a beautiful juice while efficiently separating the fiber. My second favorite would be the Champion juicer. Both are easy to use and to clean. Both can also make fruit creams! All juice recipes yield approximately 16 oz. of juice.

LIVER LOVER

The health of our liver is vital to our well-being. The liver is arguably the hardest working organ in our body. She helps to filter everything we take in, including air pollution and toxins. Beets and carrots are known to support the health of the liver. Beets especially, are deeply nourishing to the liver. So make this when you are feeling ready for some liver love.

Ingredients
- 1 large beet
- 2 medium carrots
- 1 large cucumber
- 1 knob of ginger (about half the size of your thumb)

Add your ingredients to your blender slowly, starting with the ginger. Drink immediately, to receive the highest level of nutrients and serve with love!

FALL DETOX

I first created this juice blend in the Fall for, yep you guessed it, a Fall detox. A chance to give the body a nice break, if even for one juice. The beet nourishes the liver, the ginger warms the digestive system, the carrots, apple, celery and cucumber bring hydration to the cells. The lemon balances the sweetness and brings high levels of vitamin C.

Ingredients
- ½ a medium beet
- 1 knob of ginger (about half the size of your thumb)
- 1½ large carrots
- 1 medium apple
- 3 ribs celery
- ½ large cucumber
- 1 Tablespoon lemon juice

Add your ingredients to your blender slowly, starting with the ginger. Drink immediately, to receive the highest level of nutrients and serve with love!

GREEN GODDESS

The Green Goddess just might make you feel like a Goddess. The sweetness of the apple, balanced with the savory hydration of cucumber, kale, basil and cilantro give this juice a perfect balance. She is full of vitamin C, along with a plethora of vitamins and minerals.

Ingredients
- 1½ medium apples
- 1 large cucumber
- 4 leaves of kale, with stems
- 1 knob of ginger (about the size of half of your thumb)
- 1 pinch of fresh cilantro
- 2-3 leaves fresh basil
- 1 Tablespoon lemon Juice

Serve with love!

BLOODY BEET

The Bloody Beet was created to both nourish and support the incredibly important microbiome. She is savory and has a bit of a Bloody Mary vibe. When you purchase fermented veggies, you will often have juice left over at the bottom of the jar, which is full of probiotics that support the gut. It's recommended to use good, organic and even local fermented veggies – or better yet make your own!

Ingredients
- 1 medium beet
- 2 large carrots
- ¼ of a red bell pepper
- 1 Tablespoon lemon juice
- 1 pinch of cilantro
- Fermented veggie juice – add to taste

Serve with love!

PURE

The Pure is purely savory and gives you a nice green experience. This is the juice one chooses when you want to feel fresh and invigorated.

Ingredients
- 1½ medium cucumbers
- 4 ribs celery
- 1 Tablespoon lemon Juice
- 4 large leaves of kale, collards or chard
- 1 pinch of mint leaves
- 3-4 basil leaves

Serve with love!

WONDER TONIC

The Wonder Tonic is the juice to choose when you want to feel fresh and spicy. The cayenne and ginger really warm the digestive tract while also gently nourishing and cleansing the body.

Ingredients
- 1 apple
- ⅓ bunch of fresh parsley
- 1 large knob of ginger
- 1 large knob of turmeric
- 2 Tablespoons lemon Juice
- 2 Tablespoons lime Juice
- ½ of a medium cucumber
- Small pinch of cayenne

Serve with love!

RADIANT HEART

The Radiant Heart is like sunshine in a glass. The sweet potato, carrot and orange give it a beautiful orange glow. This juice is sweet and cheerful and full of minerals and nutrients.

Ingredients
- 1½ medium apples
- ¼ cup diced or a few small pieces of sweet potato
- 1 knob of ginger
- 1 large carrot
- 2 whole and peeled oranges

Serve with love!

PLAYFUL SOUL

The Playful Soul was named after a beloved boutique that was once in the building connected to our café. This is one of our blended juices – a juice blended with some frozen fruit. A lovely sweet treat!

First, juice the following:

- 1 peeled orange
- 1 knob of ginger

Add the juice and the following to your blender:

- 1½ cups frozen pineapple
- 1 peeled orange
- 1 pinch of cilantro
- 1 Tablespoon lemon Juice
- 1 Tablespoon lime Juice
- Small pinch of cayenne

Blend and serve with love!

TUMMY TIME

A blended juice created to soothe a tummy. The warming of the ginger and turmeric combined with pineapple, helps support the digestive system. The ginger and turmeric blends well with the creaminess of the bananas and coconut mylk.

First, juice the following:

- ½ medium apple
- 1 large carrot
- 1 knob of ginger
- 1 small piece of turmeric

Add the juice and the following to your blender:

- 1¼ frozen bananas
- ¼ cup frozen pineapple chunks
- ¼ cup coconut mylk
- 1 Tablespoon lime juice

Blend and serve with love!

TUES-FRI – 8-3   BREAKFAST • LUNCH • DESSERTS – SAT/SUN 10

Ezra's
enlightened café

#ENLIGHTENYOURPLATE
WWW.EZRASENLIGHTENEDCAFE.COM

CHAPTER

2

NUT "MYLKS"

Nut mylks can be a Godsend for those who cannot handle dairy. Having fresh mylk to make smoothies, hot drinks and desserts is a beautiful thing. We loved being able to make dairy free creamy treats for folks who had dairy allergies.

There is much debate about the harm nut mylks cause to the environment and I do agree with some of those opinions. At Ezra's Café, we always, ALWAYS used organic nuts and coconut for our mylks. This was not something we were willing to compromise on.

The farming of almonds is known to be problematic for the environment for sure, so that is something to consider. Making sure the nuts you are using are organic, does help to support cleaner farming. For most of us, almonds are not local and I prefer to keep my diet for myself and my family as local as possible. These are things to look at and consider. I've always said, the label "VEGAN" does not make a person more environmentally responsible. We must look closer into the details.

At Ezra's Café, we used the leftover pulp from making almond mylk to make our pizza crusts, breads and bagels. We didn't waste anything. We also used the coconut pulp when possible to make dessert crusts. How we honor our food is so important. There are rarely perfect answers to food when the environmental impact is considered, but we can do our best to honor what we do use.

Grocery store nut mylks and seed mylks are often laden with pesticides, along with preservatives, which aren't healthy for our precious bodies. Making your own mylks, gives you freedom to choose the quality and freshness and THAT is worth the small amount of time and work it takes to make your own mylks.

ALMOND MYLK

Ingredients
- 1 cup organic almonds
- 3 cups filtered water

Directions
1. Blend your almonds and water on high until you see white bubbly mylk form. It takes about 30 seconds.
2. Now it's time to strain. Pour your mylk in the nut mylk bag over a large bowl. Gently squeeze out the mylk into the bowl.
3. What you have now is a beautiful, white almond mylk and a bag of almond pulp. You can save the pulp by freezing it in a Ziplock bag and using it later for recipes such as the bagels in this cookbook.
4. Your mylk will last up to a week in the refrigerator. You can also freeze your mylk in ice cube trays to use mylk cubes at a later date.

   Hint – add a few dates before you blend for a sweeter mylk!

COCONUT MYLK

Ingredients
- 1 cup shredded coconut
- 3 cups filtered water

Directions
1. Blend your shredded coconut and water on high until you see white bubbly mylk form. It takes about 30 seconds.
2. Now it's time to strain. Pour your mylk in the nut mylk bag over a large bowl. Gently squeeze out the mylk into the bowl.
3. What you have now is a beautiful, white coconut mylk and a bag of coconut pulp. You can save the pulp by freezing it in a Ziplock bag and using it later for recipes, such as cookies. You can also use the dehydrated pulp in place of coconut flour.
4. Your mylk will last up to a week in the refrigerator. You can also freeze your mylk in ice cube trays to use mylk cubes at a later date.

CHAPTER

3

SMOOTHIES AND ICE CREAMS

One of the offerings Ezra's Café was best known for was our smoothies. Part of our menu offerings from day one, our smoothies were always thick and filling, while being 100% free of the weird flavorings and syrups you see being used in many chain eateries. There is absolutely no need for added sugar or ice in a smoothie, if you make it with intention and preparation.

One of the main secrets of our smoothies was the use of frozen ripe bananas. If you ever graced our doors and peeked into the kitchen, it's very possible you might have seen a team member peeling bananas. We ordered cases each week and had a freezer completely dedicated to frozen bananas. These ripe bananas (always organic) provided the perfect sweetness and creaminess for our smoothies. The ripe bananas are also higher in vitamins and potassium as they ripen.

Using frozen fruit, there is never a need for added ice or sugar in a smoothie.

Smoothies can be a truly awesome way to fit in a plethora of mineral and vitamin-rich offerings like Spirulina, bee pollen, hemp seeds or even CBD oil.

We also loved having ice cream on the menu. What a delight it is for folks to experience creamy cold ice cream without the dairy, and also without the fillers and preservatives found in much of the non-dairy ice cream in grocery stores. All smoothie recipes yield approximately 16 oz.

SEDUCTION CRUMBLE

This is the crumble you'll see mentioned for the Strawberry Seduction smoothie and the Enchanted Goddess smoothie bowl. You could also use this crumble just to snack on, put over some yogurt or even make into cookie balls.

Ingredients
- ¾ cup almonds
- ½ cup oats
- 1 cup dates
- 1½ Tablespoons coconut sugar
- Less than ½ Teaspoon sea salt

Directions
1. In your food processor, add your almonds and process a few times.
2. Now add your oats, coconut sugar and sea salt and process a few times more.
3. Lastly, add your dates and process until coarse to fine consistency.

STRAWBERRY SEDUCTION

Adding this smoothie to our menu was a game changer. She's more of a dessert in smoothie form. So darn delicious! Who can resist the strawberry and chocolate combination?

Ingredients
- 2 cups frozen strawberries
- 3 pitted dates
- 1 Tablespoon maple syrup
- ½ Teaspoon vanilla extract
- 1 Tablespoon seduction crumble
- 1 cup almond mylk

Directions
1. Blend all ingredients until smooth.
2. Before serving, drizzle the inside of the cup with our chocolate sauce then pour in the smoothie.
3. Top with more chocolate sauce and enjoy this decadent smoothie with a full heart.

BUDDHA BELLY

Absolutely one of our most popular smoothies, the Buddha Belly is creamy chocolaty goodness. She brings happiness to your heart!

Ingredients
- 3 frozen bananas
- ¼ Teaspoon cinnamon
- 1 Tablespoon cacao powder
- 1 Tablespoon cacao nibs
- 1 Tablespoon almond butter
- 1 cup almond mylk

Directions
1. Blend all ingredients until smooth.
2. Top with cacao nibs and serve with love!

PROTEIN WARRIOR

This smoothie is high in protein without the use of a protein powder. A little chocolaty, sweet and a little fruity.

Ingredients

- 1½ frozen bananas
- ½ cup blueberries
- 1 Teaspoon spirulina
- ¼ Teaspoon cinnamon
- 1 Tablespoon cacao powder
- 1 Tablespoon almond butter
- 1 cup almond mylk

Blend all ingredients until smooth and serve with love!

MARY'S BERRIES

Named after a very special lady in my life, Mary's Berries was a true favorite. Very sweet and very fruity.

Ingredients
- 1½ frozen bananas
- 5 pieces frozen pineapple
- ⅓ cup frozen blueberries
- 1 Tablespoon Sun Warrior protein powder
- 1 Tablespoon almond butter
- 1 cup coconut mylk

Blend all ingredients until smooth and serve with love!

BERRY NICE

Another fruity smoothie with more of the traditional berry flavor.

- 1½ frozen bananas
- ½ cup frozen strawberries
- ¼ cup frozen blueberries
- 1 Teaspoon Sun Warrior protein powder
- ½ cup coconut mylk
- ½ cup water

Blend all ingredients until smooth and serve with love!

PINEAPPLE EXPRESS

For those who love pineapple and mango!

- 1½ frozen bananas
- ¼ cup frozen pineapple
- ¼ cup frozen mango
- 1 Teaspoon coconut oil
- 1 Tablespoon fresh chopped cilantro
- 1 Tablespoon chopped fresh mint
- 1 cup water

Blend all ingredients until smooth and serve with love!

CHERRY LOVE

Are you a cherry flavor person? This smoothie is for you, love.

- 1½ frozen bananas
- ½ cup frozen pineapple
- ½ cup frozen cherries
- ½ cup coconut mylk
- ½ cup water

Blend all ingredients until smooth and serve with love!

HEY JOE!

Are you looking for a smoothie with a pick-me-up? Chocolate and coffee…what could be better?

- 1 frozen banana
- 8 coffee ice cubes
- 1 Tablespoon cacao powder
- ½ Teaspoon cinnamon
- 1 Tablespoon maple syrup
- 3 pitted dates
- ¾ cup coconut mylk

Blend all ingredients until smooth and serve with love!

MINT CHIP SHAKE

This smoothie was a special menu offering that came around every Spring. If you love that mint chocolate combination, this is your smoothie!

- 1½ frozen banana
- ⅓ cup cashews
- 2 Tablespoons cacao nibs
- ½ Teaspoon spirulina
- ½ Teaspoon mint extract
- 2 Tablespoons fresh mint leaves
- 3 drops vanilla stevia
- 1 cup almond mylk

Blend all ingredients until smooth and serve with love!

ICE CREAM

Equipment needed: Blender, spatula, knife, cutting board, and measuring spoons

Ice cream can be made with just two ingredients! You don't need all the fillers and preservatives. And this is a very affordable way to do it, as bananas are the most inexpensive fruit at the grocery store.

ICE CREAM SUNDAE

Ice Cream Ingredients
- 2½ frozen bananas
- ¼ cup coconut mylk

Topping Ingredients
- 3 organic strawberries, sliced
- 1 Teaspoon cacao nibs
- Drizzle of chocolate sauce

Directions
1. In your blender, start with your frozen bananas and then add in coconut mylk, starting with ¼ cup. This is really best made in a high speed blender, like a Vita-Mix, where you can use a tamper.
2. As it blends, tamp down until the bananas turn into a frozen creamy ice cream. Add more coconut mylk, as needed, as you blend.
3. Scrape into your bowl and top with your favorite ingredients.
4. Serve with love!

BROWNIE ICE CREAM SUNDAE

This has all the same ingredients as the Ice Cream Sundae, but with super rich chocolate brownies to top it off. Ooooh ya!

Ice Cream Ingredients
- 2½ frozen bananas
- ¼ cup coconut mylk

Topping Ingredients
- Three organic strawberries, sliced
- 1 Teaspoon cacao nibs
- Drizzle of chocolate sauce
- 1 Triple Chocolate Brownie, cut into 4 small squares

Directions
1. In your blender, start with your frozen bananas and then add in coconut mylk, starting with ¼ cup. This is really best made in a high speed blender, like a Vita-Mix, where you can use a tamper.
2. As it blends, tamp down until the bananas turn into a frozen creamy ice cream. Add more coconut mylk as needed, as you blend.
3. Scrape into your bowl and top with your favorite ingredients, including the delicious brownie squares.
4. Serve with love!

CHAPTER

4

HERBAL TONIC LATTES, ELIXIR SHOTS & SPECIALTY DRINKS

I knew when I opened Ezra's Café that we would have an Herbal Tonic menu. I learned the magic of making Herbal Tonics when studying Chinese tonic herbs years ago with Ron Teeguarden of Dragon Herbs. The herbs used in the lattes we sold have been used for centuries and have known benefits for the body, mind and soul.

I often wonder what the world would be like if every restaurant put the well-being of the customer first before anything else. This was the reason for adding these offerings on our menu. We introduced the idea of using Reishi and Chaga among so many other mushrooms and herbs to our customer base.

The Herbal Tonic Lattes in particular, are made with powders, like pearl, reishi and some are powder mixes, such as "Awaken the Shen." We used our powders exclusively from our friends at Jing Herbs. They have been providing these mushroom and medicinal powders since before this became trendy. You can find them at https://jingherbs.com/

The drops and tinctures used for the Elixir shots are exclusively from our friends at Dragon Herbs. You can find them at https://www.dragonherbs.com/

VANILLA SWEET DREAM

I created this herbal latte to help relax the nervous system and to feel like you are being transported to a roaring fireplace with knitted mittens and snow falling outside. I remember one particular experience with this drink. A customer who was a regular, came in and inquired about our latte menu. She told me she had trouble relaxing. I recommended the Vanilla Sweet Dream. Within minutes of taking a few sips, she quietly sat down at a table and remained there for probably an hour, just sipping. She told me before she left, the latte brought her to a calm place she hadn't felt in a long time. Now, this isn't necessarily what everyone will feel but this story demonstrates the power the right herb combination can have on someone. This was just what her body needed at that moment.

Ingredients
- 1 Teaspoon Awaken the Shen
- ½ Teaspoon pearl powder
- ½ Teaspoon reishi powder
- 1 Tablespoon coconut sugar
- 5 drops of vanilla stevia
- ½ cup frothed almond mylk
- 1 cup hot water (about 190 degrees)

Directions
1. Fill your cup with your powders, stevia and coconut sugar.
2. Now pour over your 1 cup of hot water.
3. Top your cup off with about ½ cup frothed almond mylk.

HOT LOVE LATTE

The name might tip you off a bit here. This latte was created to invoke feelings of bliss and yes, even a libido boost. The deep chocolate flavor paired with the cayenne pepper, warms the body and provides that feeling of bliss that is just so delicious.

Ingredients
- ½ Teaspoon reishi powder
- ½ Teaspoon chaga powder
- ½ Teaspoon cistanche powder
- 1 Teaspoon cacao powder
- Pinch of cayenne powder
- 1 Tablespoon coconut sugar
- ½ Tablespoon coconut oil
- 3 drops vanilla stevia
- 1 Tablespoon Dandy Blend
- ½ cup frothed almond mylk
- 1 cup hot water (about 190 degrees)

Directions
1. Fill your cup with your powders, stevia, coconut sugar, coconut oil and Dandy Blend.
2. Now pour over your 1 cup hot water.
3. Top your cup off with about ½ cup frothed almond mylk.
4. Top with a chocolate sauce swirl and a sprinkle of cinnamon.

HAPPY HOT CACAO

This was our take on the traditional hot chocolate, but packed with herbs that boost the body's natural energy source. Chocolaty goodness with a purpose.

Ingredients
- ½ Teaspoon chaga powder
- ½ Teaspoon Restore the Jing powder
- ½ Teaspoon reishi powder
- 1 Tablespoon coconut sugar
- 1 Tablespoon Dandy Blend
- 1 Teaspoon cacao powder
- 5 drops of vanilla stevia
- ½ cup frothed almond mylk
- 1 cup hot water (about 190 degrees)

Directions
1. Fill your cup with your powders, stevia, coconut sugar, cacao powder and Dandy Blend.
2. Now pour over your 1 cup hot water.
3. Top cup off with about ½ cup frothed almond mylk.
4. Top with a chocolate sauce swirl and a sprinkle of cinnamon.

CHAI LOVE LATTE

This is a simple chai latte with energy support from some special herbs. For those that love that creamy chai-like experience!

Ingredients
- 1 Teaspoon Activate the Qi powder
- ¼ Teaspoon astragalus powder
- ¼ Teaspoon ginseng powder
- ⅛ Teaspoon cardamom
- ⅛ Teaspoon cinnamon
- 1 Tablespoon coconut sugar
- ½ cup frothed almond mylk
- 1 cup hot water (about 190 degrees)

Directions
1. Fill your cup with your powders and coconut sugar.
2. Now pour over your 1 cup hot water.
3. Top your cup off with about ½ cup frothed almond mylk.

GOLDEN MYLK TONIC

We created this option for those looking for the golden mylk experience that had become so popular. The turmeric and ginger really give this latte a warming experience. The black pepper helps the body absorb the benefits of the turmeric and the clove supports digestion and gives it that unique holiday-like flavor.

Ingredients
- ½ Tablespoon coconut sugar
- ½ Tablespoon honey
- ¼ Teaspoon turmeric powder
- ¼ Teaspoon ginger powder
- ¼ Teaspoon Sun Warrior vanilla protein powder
- ¼ Teaspoon cinnamon
- Pinch of black pepper
- Pinch of clove powder
- 1 cup boiling water (about 190 degrees)
- ½ cup frothed coconut mylk

Directions
1. Fill your cup with your powders and coconut sugar.
2. Now pour over your 1 cup of hot water and stir.
3. Drizzle in your honey and stir again.
4. Top your cup off with about ½ cup frothed almond mylk.

NAMASTE COFFEE

Our take on the popular bullet-proof coffee trend with a touch of Ayurvedic-inspired spices.

Ingredients
- 1½ cups hot coffee
- ¼ cup coconut mylk
- 1 Teaspoon coconut oil
- 1 Teaspoon coconut sugar
- ¼ Teaspoon cardamom powder
- ¼ Teaspoon ginger powder
- ¼ Teaspoon cinnamon

Directions
1. Add your coconut mylk, coconut oil, coconut sugar and spices to your blender and blend until combined.
2. Add your mix to your cup and then pour over your hot coffee. Stir with a spoon and enjoy.

ICED COFFEE

For those who love a good iced coffee, this is incredibly simple. We used high quality organic and fair trade strong black coffee.

Ingredients
- Coffee ice cubes
- Chilled coffee
- Almond mylk

Directions
Fill your cup with coffee cubes then add as much mylk as you desire, and then top off with your chilled coffee.

GINGER TURMERIC IMMUNE BOOST

This shot was on our menu from day one at Ezra's Café. I knew I wanted a super potent shot that would help prevent sickness and treat it as well. This shot remained one of our most popular items on the menu until the day we closed. We had customers that would purchase multiple shots at a time to take home for the cold and flu season. The stories of folks who said it helped give them energy, treat the flu, cold, headaches and more accumulated over the years. Ginger is incredibly good at killing viruses. Turmeric helps to deal with inflammation and the lemon brings in the high level of Vitamin C and antioxidants. The honey soothes the throat and also brings in more antioxidants and anti-bacterial power.

Ingredients
- Fresh ginger root
- Fresh turmeric root
- Fresh Lemons
- Raw local honey

Directions

1. To make your Immune Boost mix, you will juice each item separately. Start with your turmeric. Juice enough to get ¼ cup of juice. It really depends on how fresh your turmeric root is as to how much you'll need to use. Pour into a jar or bowl with enough room to add more juice.
2. Next, juice your ginger root until you have ¼ cup of juice. Add this juice to the bowl with the turmeric juice.
3. Lastly, juice your lemons until you have ½ cup. We liked to juice the whole lemon, which brings in the zest, which is extremely high in Vitamin C and antioxidants. Add your lemon juice to the bowl.
4. Mix your juice with a spoon to combine.
5. Now pour yourself a shot, adding raw honey to the shot glass, if you desire. This juice is very spicy, so start with a sip!
6. Your mix will last up to a month in an air-tight container in your refrigerator.

EMPEROR'S SECRET

I created this shot for those suffering from a headache. We had many customers tell us it truly worked. Headaches are tricky and can be caused by so many things so it might not always work, but it's worth a shot! This shot also helps to bring in relaxation.

Ingredients
- 3 oz. of your favorite bubbly kombucha
- 15 drops of CBD oil (we used the Signature concentrated line from Bluebird Botanicals, which is approximately 0.5 ml of CBD per 15 drops)
- 15 drops of Shen tincture from Dragon Herbs

Directions
In a small cup or shot glass, add your kombucha and then top with your CBD and Shen tincture. You can also use a Reishi tincture of your choice in place of the Shen.

BLISSFUL YOU

We exclusively used Dragon Herbs tinctures and Spring Dragon tea at Ezra's Café. However, you can use the brands of tincture and any tea that you desire. Reishi uplifts the heart and ginseng uplifts the energy.

Ingredients
- 18 drops reishi tincture
- 18 drops ginseng tincture
- 2 oz. of warm or hot tea

Directions
Add your tinctures to your small cup or shot of tea and sip!

DIAMOND MIND

Dragon Herbs has a tincture blend called Diamond Mind, which of course is the inspiration for the name of this shot. The Diamond Mind tincture supports brain function.

Ingredients
- 36 drops Diamond Mind tincture from Dragon Herbs
- 2 oz. of warm or hot tea

Directions
Add your tinctures to your small cup or shot of tea and sip!

LUMINOUS GLOW

Schizandra and Goji tincture is known to support the liver and thus the skin.

Ingredients
- 36 drops of Schizandra & Goji drops from Dragon Herbs
- 2 oz. of warm or hot tea

Directions
Add your tinctures to your small cup or shot of tea and sip!

VIBRANT HEALTH

Duanwood Reishi tincture is known to support overall well-being

Ingredients
- 36 drops of Duanwood Reishi tincture from Dragon Herbs
- 2 oz. of warm or hot tea

Directions
Add your tinctures to your small cup or shot of tea and sip!

GIN AND JUICE

This shot helps to rev up digestion and provide a kick of energy.

Ingredients
- 3 large leaves of kale (with stem)
- 1 small knob of ginger
- 1 Teaspoon lemon juice or ¼ of a lemon

Directions
Juice your ingredients, starting with your ginger. Drink to your health!

BRAIN ON

We used E3 Live products from day one at Ezra's Café. They offer high potent green powders and their Brain On powder is a concentrated blend that supports, you guessed it, the brain. Both concentration and memory.

Ingredients
- 1 scoop (they provide a scooper in the jar) or ¼ teaspoon Brain On
- 2 oz. warm or hot tea

Directions
Add your powder to your hot tea, stir and shoot. This isn't a super yummy shot, so it's meant to shoot quickly.

HAPPY GUT

We used only local organic fermented veggies at Ezra's Café. We ended up sourcing the most amazing blend in our last few years from our friends Megan and Joe who make the most potent and mineral-rich fermented foods. There is always the juice left behind and this is potent medicine for the gut.

Ingredients
- 2 oz. of fermented veggie juice
- ¼ Teaspoon lemon juice

Directions
Pour both the fermented veggie juice and lemon juice into a cup. Stir and sip. Cheers to your happy gut!

CHAPTER
5

SMOOTHIE AND GRANOLA BOWLS

Our smoothie and granola bowls were a favorite for so many of our customers. As the years progressed, we added more smoothie bowls and they became one of the most popular items on our menu. Some days our Juice Bar person could barely keep up! The amount of frozen bananas we went through, let me tell you.

There is just something about a smoothie bowl that delights the taste buds and the soul. We topped our bowls with organic crunchy pistachios, hemp seeds and our home-made granola. You can add just about anything you like on a smoothie bowl – that's the best part! A smoothie bowl is a beautiful way to bring in a deep level of nutrients in a tasty treat.

Our granola bowls were created to be simple yet highly delicious. A nod to the cereals that many of us grew up eating. We now know those boxed cereals were not only void of nutrients but often full of sugars, seed oils and worse. Granola bowls are a beautiful way to have that cereal-like experience with deep nutrients and none of the yuck from boxed cereals.

RISING WARRIOR SMOOTHIE BOWL

Smoothie Ingredients
- 1¾ bananas
- 2 Tablespoons frozen blueberries
- ½ Tablespoon Sun Warrior vanilla protein powder (or your favorite vanilla protein powder)
- 1 Teaspoon spirulina
- ¼ Teaspoon cinnamon
- ½ Tablespoon almond butter
- ¼ cup almond mylk

Place all of your smoothie ingredients into your blender and blend until smooth.

Pour your smoothie into your favorite bowl and top with the following:

- ½ cup Lime Buckwheat Granola
- ⅔ sliced banana
- 1 Tablespoon almond butter
- 1 Tablespoon chopped pistachios
- ½ Teaspoon hemp seeds
- 1 pinch of local bee pollen

Serve with love!

ENCHANTED GODDESS SMOOTHIE BOWL

Ingredients (you are basically making a half of a Strawberry Seduction)
- 2 cups frozen strawberries
- 2 dried and pitted dates
- 1 Tablespoon maple syrup
- ½ Teaspoon vanilla extract
- 1 Teaspoon Seduction Crumble
- ¼ cup almond mylk

Place all of your smoothie ingredients into your blender and blend until smooth.

Pour your smoothie into your favorite bowl and top with the following:

- 3-4 sliced fresh organic strawberries
- 2 tablespoons seduction crumble
- Drizzle of chocolate sauce

Serve with love!

ASCENDED WARRIOR SMOOTHIE BOWL

Ingredients
- 1½ frozen bananas
- 2 Tablespoons frozen blueberries
- 3 large chunks of frozen pineapple
- ½ Tablespoon almond butter
- ¼ cup coconut mylk

Place all of your smoothie ingredients into your blender and blend until smooth.

Pour your smoothie into your favorite bowl and top with the following:

- ½ cup Chili Chocolate Granola
- 3-4 fresh organic sliced strawberries
- 1 Tablespoon almond butter
- 1 Tablespoon chopped pistachios
- ½ Teaspoon hemp seeds
- Pinch (maybe 10 or so) goji berries

Serve with love!

BAREFOOT BANANA BOWL

Ingredients
- 2 frozen bananas
- ½ Teaspoon cinnamon
- ¼ Teaspoon Sun Warrior vanilla protein powder
- ¼ cup coconut mylk

Place all of your smoothie ingredients into your blender and blend until smooth.

Pour your smoothie into your favorite bowl and top with the following:

- ⅔ fresh banana, sliced
- ⅓ cup Carrot Spice Muffin, crumbled
- ½ Teaspoon hemp seeds
- 1 date, diced
- Sprinkle of cinnamon

Serve with love!

MORNING SYNERGY BOWL

Ingredients
- 1 Carrot Spice Muffin
- 1 cup mylk of your choice
- ½ of a banana, sliced
- 1 Teaspoon goji berries

Directions
1. Crumble your muffin into your favorite bowl.
2. Pour over your mylk of choice.
3. Now top with your slices of banana and goji berries.
4. Enjoy with a full heart!

LIME BUCKWHEAT GRANOLA BOWL

Ingredients
- 1¼ cup of your Lime Buckwheat Granola
- 1 cup mylk of your choice
- ½ banana, sliced
- 1 Teaspoon goji berries
- ½ Teaspoon local bee pollen

Directions
1. Add as much granola as you like into your bowl.
2. Pour over your mylk of choice.
3. Now top with your slices of banana and goji berries.
4. Enjoy with a full heart!

CHILI CHOCOLATE GRANOLA BOWL

Ingredients
- 1¼ cup of your Chili Chocolate Granola
- 1 cup mylk of your choice
- ½ banana, sliced
- 1 Teaspoon goji berries
- ½ Teaspoon local bee pollen

Directions
1. Add as much granola as you like into your bowl.
2. Pour over your mylk of choice.
3. Now top with your slices of banana and goji berries.
4. Enjoy with a full heart!

CHAPTER

6

GRANOLA AND SNACKS

We loved offering packaged snacks for our customers to take home. The granolas we used for our granola bowls, and to top smoothie bowls, were packaged up for our customers to enjoy at home.

Our kale chips flew off the shelf so fast they often lasted only hours. Many customers told us they were the best kale chips they've ever had. We have a few tricks to show you in the recipes that ensure you get the crunchiest and most delicious taste in each bite.

LIME BUCKWHEAT GRANOLA

Equipment needed: Food processor, dehydrator and Teflex sheets, grater for zesting limes, measuring cups and spoons, large bowl

This granola is nut-free and created to be very digestible, light yet full of flavor.

Ingredients
- 10 cups buckwheat (soaked)
- ¼ cup lime zest
- 2½ Tablespoons lime juice
- ¾ Teaspoon sea salt
- ½ cup date paste
- 1 cup maple syrup
- 1 Tablespoon vanilla
- 2 cups raisins
- 2½ cups coconut flakes

Directions

1. Soak your buckwheat overnight in fresh filtered water – add enough water to be 2 inches above your buckwheat.
2. Now, it's the next day and time to rinse your buckwheat. You want to remove as much of the mucilage (the sliminess) as you can. I like to rinse well in a large strainer.
3. To make date paste: process 3 cups dates, 1 cup water, and 1½ cups maple syrup in the food processor. This will give you more than you need for this recipe. You can double this recipe, use the extra for something else or even freeze it.
4. Next, you'll want to zest your limes.
5. In a large metal bowl, mix your buckwheat along with all ingredients, including your date paste. Mix well so that your buckwheat, raisins and coconut are well coated.
6. Dehydrate on your dehydrator sheet with Teflex for at least 8 hours or until completely dry.

CHILI CHOCOLATE GRANOLA

Equipment needed: Large bowl, small bowl, spatula, measuring cups and spoons, dehydrator and Teflex sheets

This granola ended up having quite the following. Enjoy the crunchy, sweet chocolaty goodness with a kick of heat.

Ingredients
- 3 cups gluten free oats
- 1 cup soaked pumpkin seeds
- 1 cup soaked almonds
- 1 cup soaked sunflower seeds
- 1 cup organic maple syrup
- ½ cup raisins
- ⅓ cup hemp seeds
- ⅓ cup shredded coconut
- ⅓ cup melted coconut oil
- ¼ cup plus 2 Tablespoons cacao powder
- 1 Tablespoon vanilla extract
- 1 Teaspoon sea salt
- ½ Teaspoon cayenne powder

Directions

1. Soak the pumpkin, sunflower seeds, and almonds overnight. Drain, rinse and add to your large bowl along with your oats, hemp seeds, raisins and shredded coconut.
2. In a second smaller bowl, measure the maple syrup, coconut oil, cacao powder, vanilla, sea salt and cayenne. Mix until combined. Pour over the seeds, nuts, oats and such in the larger bowl.
3. Mix well with a spatula and eventually with your hands. It will be a bit messy but you really want to make sure everything is well coated. And, you can lick your fingers after, if you like.
4. Spread your mixture on your dehydrator trays so that it's about an inch thick. Use your Teflex sheets, if you have them, to keep the dripping of any syrup to a minimum while it dries. Dehydrate at 115 degrees for 12-24 hours until completely dry.
5. Your granola will last months if kept cool and dry.

SPICY CHEEZY KALE CHIPS

Equipment needed: Blender, large bowl, cutting board, knife, measuring cups and spoons, dehydrator and Teflex sheets

If anything sold out quickly, it was our packages of these chips. We could barely keep them on the shelf. That combination of rich, salty, sweet and crunchy made quite possibly the perfect snack.

Ingredients
- 3 Bunches of fresh kale

Cheezy mix
- 3 cups of cashews
- 3 chopped red bell peppers
- ½ Teaspoon cayenne
- 3 Tablespoons nutritional yeast
- 3 Teaspoons sea salt
- 1½ Teaspoons maple syrup

Topping
- ¼ cup sesame seeds

Directions
1. First, you want to wash and strip your kale. Basically, you will strip the leaves off of the stems. Don't break up into small pieces, as you want them as large as possible because they will shrink.
2. In your blender, starting with red bell peppers, add all cheezy mix ingredients and blend until smooth.
3. Pour your cheezy mix over your kale in a large bowl and massage kale until completely saturated. This helps to break down the cell walls of the kale and also ensures every part of your chips are evenly coated.
4. Lay out the cheezy kale onto a dehydrator tray with a Teflex sheet.
5. Sprinkle 2-4 Tablespoons of sesame seeds all over the cheezy kale.
6. Dehydrate at 120° for 12 hours or until completely dry and enjoy!

HONEY SPICED KALE CHIPS

Equipment needed: Blender, large bowl, cutting board, knife, spatula, measuring cups and spoons, dehydrator and Teflex sheets

If you love the combination of sweet and salty, these chips are right up your alley.

Ingredients
- 3-4 large bunches of kale

Honey Spice Dressing
- ½ cup olive oil
- ⅓ cup raw local honey
- 1¼ Teaspoon sea salt
- ¼ Teaspoon cayenne

Topping
- ½ cup sesame seeds

To process kale:
De-stem the kale by holding with one hand and quickly pulling upward, allowing your thumb and pointer finger to act as a ring, stripping the leaves. The stems can go into compost or you can even juice them.

Directions
1. Fill 1 large metal bowl with your washed and stripped kale.
2. Add your dressing ingredients into a separate small metal bowl and whisk together until as combined as possible. You will see that the oil and honey will stay somewhat separate, which is okay.
3. Pour on top of your bowl of kale and mix with your hands. Massage kale with your hands until the dressing is evenly distributed. This massaging helps to break down the cell walls of the kale.
4. Place your dressed kale on your dehydrator sheets with Teflex, in one layer, ensuring the kale has room to dry.
5. Sprinkle kale with sesame seeds, ensuring every piece has seeds on it.
6. Dehydrate kale at 120° for 6 hours or until completely dry.

ALFREDO KALE CHIPS

Equipment needed: Blender, measuring cups and spoons, spatula, dehydrator trays, Teflex sheets, medium-large metal bowl

Our Alfredo Kale Chips were not a regular menu item but when we did make them, they sold out right away. Decadence in a chip!

Sauce Ingredients
- 4 cups cashews
- 1¼ cups of fresh basil, packed
- 1 clove garlic
- ¼ cup nutritional yeast
- 2 Tablespoons chickpea miso
- 3 Tablespoons lemon juice
- 1 Teaspoon coriander
- 1 Tablespoon dried thyme
- ½ cup olive oil
- 2 cups water

- 3 bunches of kale, washed, destemmed and dried
- 2 Tablespoons Walnut Parm

Directions
1. Blend all sauce ingredients until smooth.
2. In a large bowl, pour your sauce over your kale.
3. Massage with your hands until every piece of kale is completely saturated with the sauce and the kale is soft.
4. Lay the dressed kale onto a dehydrator tray with a Teflex sheet.
5. Sprinkle 1-2 Tablespoons of your Walnut Parm over all of the dressed kale.
6. Dehydrate at 115 degrees for 20-24 hours.
7. Package into a sealed glass container and keep in a cool dry space and they will last for a few months.

ZESTY TOMATO BASIL FLAX CRACKERS

Each tray will make about 25 crackers

Equipment needed: Blender, measuring cups, offset spatula, dehydrator trays, Teflex sheets, medium-large metal bowl for soaking flax seeds

These crackers are incredibly satisfying. The flavor of the herbs and tomato really pop. Having a batch on hand saves you when you are looking for the crunch without the fillers from grocery store crackers.

Ingredients
- 2 cups flax seeds, soaked
- 4 cups water
- 2 tomatoes, chopped
- 3 cloves garlic
- ½ small yellow onion
- ½ cup ground flax seeds
- 2 Teaspoons dried oregano
- 1 Teaspoon chili powder
- ¼ cup chopped fresh basil
- 1 Teaspoon sea salt

Directions
1. Soak your flax in 4 cups of water overnight or for at least 4 hours. Stir before using, as seeds will become gelatinous.
2. Add your tomatoes, garlic, onion, oregano, chili powder and salt to your high-speed blender and process until slightly chunky. Add in your basil and blend until smooth.
3. Pour the tomato mixture and ground flax seeds into the soaked flax and stir until completely combined.
4. Add 3 cups of your cracker mixture onto your Teflex sheet, if you are using an Excalibur. In general, you want about ¼ inch of mix or so covering your sheet. Smooth to the edges of your tray and score with the edge of your spatula.
5. Dehydrate at 110 for approximately 24 hours.
6. Flip the crackers over onto the mesh surface without the Teflex sheet, which will allow the air to circulate around both sides of crackers. Dehydrate more until completely dry.

CURRIED SUNFLOWER SEEDS

Equipment needed: Bowl, measuring spoons and cups, dehydrator and Teflex sheets

Having these on hand makes it easy to add crunch and flavor to your favorite veggie bowl. They are also the perfect travel snack.

Ingredients
- 2½ cups sunflower seeds
- 3 Tablespoons raw local honey
- 1 Teaspoon sea salt
- 2 Tablespoons curry powder
- ½ Tablespoon turmeric powder

Directions
1. Measure out sunflower seeds and soak for at least 4 hours or overnight – make sure water is a couple of inches over the seeds.
2. Drain and rinse your sunflower seeds.
3. Add all of your ingredients to your sunflower seeds in a bowl and mix well with a large spoon or your hands.
4. Lay your seeds over a dehydrator tray with Teflex sheet and dehydrate at 115° for at least 15 hours or until completely dry.

Store your seeds in a glass container, in a cool dry place for up to 6 months or longer.

CHAPTER
7

SAUCES AND DRESSINGS

A sauce or dressing can make or break a dish. It's so important to know how to balance a dressing or a sauce to hit many of those flavor points on the tongue.

So many of the sauces and dressings you find bottled in the grocery store are riddled with seed oils, sugar and preservatives. We never used seed oils in our dressings! It's challenging to find a restaurant these days that will use organic olive oil in their sauces or dressings. Canola is often used because it's so much cheaper. The health of our customers was always our number one priority. Especially when it came to the oils and nuts we used to make our sauces and dressings.

The Lemon Tahini and Nacho Cheeze sauces were by far our most popular and loved dressing/sauce. I am so happy to be able to provide these recipes so that you can now make them at home!

LEMON GARLIC TAHINI DRESSING

Equipment needed: Blender, measuring cups and spoons, knife, cutting board

This is the dressing that became a favorite of thousands of customers over the years, originally served with our Buddha Bowl but became so popular, we also sold it separately.

Ingredients
- ½ cup tahini
- ½ cup water
- ¼ cup lemon Juice
- 2 cloves garlic
- ½ Teaspoon sea salt
- 2 Tablespoons raw honey
- 1 pinch of cumin
- 1 pinch of cayenne

Directions
Put all ingredients in your blender and blend well until combined. This dressing will last for 5-7 days in your refrigerator.

NACHO CHEEZE SAUCE

Equipment needed: Blender, knife, cutting board, measuring cups and spoons

Talk about a cult following. This cheeze was one of the most requested items we sold. We had many customers who asked for extra or wanted to purchase containers of this loved cheeze. We made it specifically for the Nacho Mama's Bean Bowl but it is truly an amazing dipping sauce for crackers or veggies or will help make the most epic nachos you've ever had.

Ingredients
- 2 large bell peppers or 2½ medium, chopped
- 3½ cup cashews
- 5 garlic cloves
- ½ Teaspoon onion powder
- ⅓ Teaspoon mustard powder
- 1½ Teaspoon turmeric
- ¼ cup nutritional yeast
- 1 Teaspoon sea salt
- 1 heaping Tablespoon tamari
- 1 Tablespoon chickpea miso
- Pinch of cayenne
- 1 heaping Teaspoon chili powder
- ¾ - 1 cup water (start with ¾)
- 1 Tablespoon lemon juice

Directions
1. Blend all ingredients together in your blender, making sure to put all of the soft ingredients like the red pepper at the bottom. By putting the soft ingredients in first, it makes it easier to blend together.
2. Make sure that you do not over heat the mixture! We just want to blend until everything is nice and smooth. You want it to be pourable but not runny.
3. Enjoy with chips, crackers, veggies, on sandwiches, as a dressing and so much more.

HERBED CASHEW CHEEZE AND SAUCE

Equipment needed: Blender, measuring cups and spoons, knife, cutting board

Cheeze ingredients
• 2 cups cashews
• 1½ cup water
• 4 garlic cloves
• 1 Tablespoon nutritional yeast
• 2 Tablespoons chickpea miso

Herb topping ingredients
• ¼ cup Pistachios
• ¼ Teaspoon sea salt
• Equal parts of 3 fresh herbs chopped: basil, thyme, rosemary, sage, or oregano – a pinch of each

Directions
1. Add all ingredients into your blender and blend until creamy. You will most likely need your tamper to keep the cheeze going, as it's supposed to be pretty thick.
2. Pour the cheeze into a container of your choice.
3. Mix the herb topping together by hand in a bowl, then add it to the top of the cheeze and serve it with love!
4. You can make this cheeze into more of a sauce by leaving the pistachios out and adding a tiny bit of water to make it more pourable.

CASHEW SOUR CREAM

Equipment needed: Blender, measuring cups and spoons, knife, cutting board

Ingredients
- 4 cups cashews
- 2 cups water
- 4 Tablespoons lemon juice
- 4 Tablespoons apple cider vinegar
- 1 Teaspoon salt

Directions
1. Blend all ingredients into a blender until smooth and glossy.
2. Your sour cream will keep in the refrigerator for up to a week. Enjoy this topping on dishes, as a sandwich spread or even a dip!

CASHEW ONION & DILL VEGGIE DIP

Equipment needed: Blender, measuring cups and spoons, knife, cutting board

Ingredients
- 2 large onions, sliced and browned
- 2 cups cashews
- ¾ cup almond mylk
- 1 Teaspoon apple cider vinegar
- ½ cup fresh dill
- 1 Teaspoon garlic powder
- ½ Teaspoon salt (more or less to taste)
- pinch of black pepper

Directions
1. First, you want to brown your onions in a pan with a bit of olive oil.
2. Next, you will blend everything, except the onions, in your blender until smooth and creamy.
3. Pulse in browned onion, allowing small chunks of onion in the dip.
4. Place into a beautiful bowl surrounded by fresh organic veggies and serve with love!

CURRY DRESSING

Equipment needed: Blender, measuring cups and spoons, knife, cutting board

Ingredients
- 3 cups olive oil
- ¾ cup maple syrup
- ¾ cup lime juice
- 1½ Tablespoons turmeric powder
- 3 Tablespoons coriander powder
- 3 Tablespoons curry powder
- ½ Tablespoon sea salt

Directions
1. Blend all ingredients until very smooth.
2. Keep in a glass jar in your refrigerator. This will keep for months!

EARTHLING DRESSING

Equipment needed: Blender, measuring cups and spoons, knife, cutting board

This dressing is quite unique, both in flavor and in color. Bright green, this is a fun one to drizzle over roasted veggies or a warm bowl of veggies, rice and beans. Whatever your heart desires! This dressing is high in minerals and immune- supporting nutrients. What a beautiful way to bring plant medicine into your daily life.

Ingredients
- 1 cup pumpkin seeds
- 2 Tablespoons apple cider vinegar
- ¼ cup olive oil
- 1 Teaspoon sea salt
- 1 knob of fresh ginger
- 1 knob of fresh turmeric
- 3 cloves of garlic, minced
- 3 Tablespoons maple syrup
- ½ cup and 1 Tablespoon filtered water
- ¼ Teaspoon cinnamon
- 1 Teaspoon spirulina

Directions
1. Blend all ingredients until very smooth.
2. Keep in a glass jar in your refrigerator for up to a week.

LEMON HERB DRESSING

Equipment Needed: Blender, measuring cups and spoons, knife, cutting board

Ingredients
- ¼ cup lemon juice
- ¼ cup olive oil
- 1 Teaspoon fresh rosemary
- 1 Teaspoon fresh sage
- 1 Teaspoon fresh mint
- 3 garlic cloves
- 1½ Teaspoons raw local honey
- ¼ Teaspoon sea salt

Directions
1. Blend all ingredients until very smooth.
2. Keep in a glass jar in your refrigerator for a month or longer.

RANCH DRESSING

Equipment needed: Blender, measuring cups and spoons, knife, cutting board

Ingredients
- 1½ cups cashews, soaked
- ½ cup + 1 Tablespoon filtered water
- 2 Tablespoons apple cider vinegar
- 4 large cloves of garlic, minced
- 1 Teaspoon raw honey
- 1 Tablespoon onion powder
- ½ Teaspoon sea salt
- 1 Tablespoon olive oil
- ½ cup minced fresh dill

Directions
1. Blend all dressing ingredients until very smooth.
2. Pour into a bowl or container and add in your minced fresh dill and gently stir.
3. Keep in a glass jar in your refrigerator for a month or longer.

DILL CASHEW CREAM CHEEZE

Equipment needed: Blender, measuring cups and spoons, knife, cutting board

Ingredients
- 4 cups soaked cashews
- 2 Teaspoons white pepper
- 1½ Teaspoons sea salt
- 2 Teaspoons apple cider vinegar
- 1½ Teaspoons garlic powder
- 1⅓ cups water
- 2 cups minced fresh dill

Directions
1. Make your cream cheeze by blending all dressing ingredients, except your dill, until very smooth.
2. Pour into a bowl or container and add in your minced fresh dill and gently stir.
3. Keep in a glass jar in your refrigerator for a month or longer.
4. This makes an absolutely delicious sandwich spread or dip for your crackers or veggies!

QUINOA BURGER SAUCE

Equipment needed: blender, measuring cups and spoons, knife, cutting board

As the name suggests, we created this sauce for our Quinoa Burger Wrap. But you can use it in any way you like, including in any wrap or as a sandwich spread.

Ingredients
- 1 cup filtered water
- ¼ cup lemon juice
- 1 Tablespoon lemon zest
- ¼ cup chopped red onion
- 1 sprig of fresh rosemary
- 1 Teaspoon cayenne pepper
- ¼ cup olive oil
- Pinch of salt to taste
- Pinch of black pepper to taste

Directions
1. Blend all ingredients until smooth and glossy.
2. Keep in a glass jar in your refrigerator for a month or longer. This is what we used inside of the Quinoa Burger Wrap at the café. You can use it as a dip or sandwich spread, or anything you like!

GARDEN HOT SAUCE

Equipment needed: Blender, measuring cups and spoons, knife, cutting board

We began making our own hot sauce when we had a nice harvest of hot peppers from our farm. From that year on, we made sure to grow enough hot peppers to supply us in Summer and well into Fall and Winter for this hot sauce our customers loved.

Ingredients
- 1½ cups chopped fresh hot peppers
- 2 Tablespoons fresh garlic
- 1 Teaspoon onion powder
- 1½ Teaspoons sea salt
- ¼ cup red onion
- ⅛ cup apple cider vinegar
- ⅛ cup coconut sugar

Directions
1. Blend all ingredients until smooth.
2. Keep it in a glass container in your fridge for up to 3 months.

CHAPTER

8

LUNCH

This chapter will give you the foundational recipes that built many of our bowls and dishes. We also include our most popular dishes that were always on the menu.

Lunch was often a time when a line would form in our small café. I loved watching people strike up conversation with folks they knew or perhaps make a new connection. Our large window housed a long bar made by my now late father. He built that bar in his shop with so much love and it then offered a place for folks to enjoy their meal. Lunch time was my favorite because it was when the café felt the most full and abundant with human interaction. I hope you enjoy these recipes and if you were a regular customer, may they bring you happy memories of our sweet space.

SLOW COOKED PINTO BEANS

Equipment needed: Crockpot, container for soaking, knife, cutting board, measuring cups and spoons

My dear friend, Corie, who was part of our opening crew at Ezra's Café, taught me her family recipe one night, in her kitchen, while our children played in the background. When I tasted her beans, a light bulb went on and I asked if we could use the recipe at Ezra's Café for our bowls. And the rest is history.

Every night before our team would close up for the day, we put our soaked beans in the slow cooker to lovingly and slowly cook overnight. In the morning, they were ready to be served to our customers.

Ingredients
- 11 cups soaked beans
- 20 cups water
- 2 tomatoes, quartered
- ½ large onion, quartered and root end removed
- 3 Tablespoons sea salt

Directions
1. Measure out 11 cups of dried pinto beans onto a clean table and pick out the beans that are old, discolored, and too shriveled. Discard the old beans. Healthy beans should look vibrant in color and in structure.
2. Soak 11 cups of beans in 20 cups of water overnight or at least 7 hours. Beans will expand as they soak up the water, so cover fully with water.
3. Rinse beans after soaking and add rinsed beans into the crockpot.
4. Add your tomatoes, onion and sea salt and put your lid on. Set the crockpot to high and cook for 8-10 hours.
5. Before refrigerating, allow your beans to cool for a few hours. You don't want to add piping hot food to the refrigerator. Your beans will keep up to a week in the refrigerator.

STEAMED ROSEMARY SWEET POTATOES

Equipment needed: Pot with steamer basket, knife, cutting board, measuring cups and spoons

We used these for our Rosemary Sweet Potato bowl, but this simple method provides such a nourishing option to add to any meal.

Ingredients
- Sweet potatoes, washed and cubed
- Fresh rosemary
- Sea salt
- Olive oil

Directions
1. Add your sweet potatoes to your steamer basket with your water boiling. Put your lid on and allow to steam until soft – about 15 minutes.
2. To dress your sweet potatoes, drizzle over your olive oil and then sprinkle with your sea salt – both to taste.
3. Lastly, sprinkle over your chopped rosemary. Gently stir and serve steaming.

HONEY SPICED KALE

Equipment needed: Blender, large bowl, small metal bowl, cutting board, knife, spatula, measuring cups and spoons

This is the kale that made our Buddha Bowl famous. I'll tell you how it happened. One day, when testing out our Honey Spiced Kale chips, they smelled so good, I started snacking on them right from the dehydrator tray before they were done. Warm and soft and so very good! I thought, wow we can use this half dehydrated kale to make a salad! We tried that for a while, but the warming of the kale was not sustainable with the amount of customers we had. We decided to simply massage the kale instead.

This became a daily morning task in our kitchen. Dressing and massaging the kale for the day's Buddha Bowls. We joked that we had the most relaxed salad in town.

Ingredients
- 3-4 large bunches of kale

Honey Spice Dressing
- ½ cup olive oil
- ⅓ cup raw local honey
- 1¼ Teaspoons sea salt
- ¼ Teaspoon cayenne

To process kale:
De-stem the kale by holding with one hand and quickly pulling upward, allowing your thumb and pointer finger to act as a ring, stripping the leaves. The stems can go into compost or you can juice them.

Directions
1. Fill a large metal bowl with your washed and stripped kale.
2. Add your dressing ingredients into a separate small metal bowl and whisk together, until as combined as possible. You will see that the oil and honey will stay somewhat separate, which is okay.
3. Pour on top of kale in the large bowl and mix with your hands. Massage kale with your hands until the dressing is evenly distributed. This massaging helps to break down the cell walls of the kale.
4. Serve in your favorite dish and enjoy!

SWEET POTATO QUINOA BURGERS

Equipment needed: Food processor, knife, cutting board, large bowl, measuring cups and spoons

These are so very flavorful. You can make these in place of a traditional burger or even as a topping for a salad or to put into a wrap. They can be served warm or cold!

Ingredients
- 4 cups cooked quinoa
- 4 cups steamed, chopped sweet potatoes
- ½ cup diced red onion
- 2 Tablespoons minced garlic
- ¾ cup chopped cilantro
- ¼ cup ground flax
- 1 cup ground oats
- 1½ cups fresh pinto beans
- 2 Teaspoons sea salt
- 3 Tablespoons lime juice
- ¼ Teaspoon white pepper

Directions
1. Combine all ingredients together in a large bowl and mix with a large spoon until thoroughly mixed.
2. Place small batches (about 2 cups) of the mixture into a food processor and process until a dough forms (stop before it becomes a paste). You want to still be able to see flecks of cilantro, quinoa and bits of onion, etc. Remove the mixture from the food processor into a bowl. Then repeat this step until you have processed all the mixture.
3. Once all of the mixture has been processed, form into patties with ½ cup of your burger mixture. Place the patties onto the dehydrator trays. Nine patties fit on one tray, if you are using an Excalibur.
4. Bake your burgers at 350° until desired consistency is reached. Try 30 minutes and then bake for longer if you want it more firm, etc. Your quinoa, beans and sweet potato are already cooked, so it's more of a matter of how you like your burger than safety.

EVERYTHING ALMOND FLAX BAGEL

Makes 9 (18 halves)

Equipment needed: Food processor, knife, measuring cups and spoons, large bowl, dehydrator

We sold these gluten-free raw bagels in our case and they were a staple for the lifetime of the café. Customers who didn't want the gluten but missed the bagel experience really loved these. You can top with whatever you desire. They are actually really lovely when toasted.

Bagel Ingredients
- 4 cups ground flax
- 3 cups almond pulp
- 3 cups zucchini puree
- 2 Teaspoons sea salt
- 2 Tablespoons olive oil
- 2 Tablespoons maple syrup
- 2 Teaspoons garlic powder
- 2 Teaspoons onion powder
- ½ cup soaked and chopped sun dried tomatoes

Topping
- ½ cup sesame seeds
- ½ cup caraway seeds

Directions
1. First, you want to make your zucchini puree. Chop your zucchini into small pieces and blend in your blender or food processor until it becomes a green smooth puree. Make a half batch at a time. One full batch doesn't fit in your food processor.
2. To make your bagel: Process flax and almond pulp until combined. Add remaining ingredients and process again until a smooth dough forms.
3. Using 1 cup measure, roll into a ball and gently create a hole, forming a smooth even bagel shape.
4. Press bagel into the sesame caraway mixture on both sides.
5. Place onto mesh sheets and dehydrate at 115° for 6 hours. Cut into half and dehydrate again for 2-3 hours until firm.
6. You can also bake these instead of dehydrating them. Bake at 300° for 1 hour, then cut in half and bake for another 45 minutes to an hour, depending on the consistency you are looking for.
7. These will need to be kept in the refrigerator or even the freezer. The inside will still be a bit moist.

HERBED FALAFELS

Makes about 37 Falafel balls

Equipment needed: Food processor, knife, measuring cups and spoons, large bowl, dehydrator

Our falafels were inspired by a recipe I learned at Living Light Culinary Institute in 2009. To this day, they are still the most amazing bean-free and "raw" falafels I've ever had. They are crispy on the outside, flavorful and filling. These falafels were part of the signature Buddha Bowl at Ezra's Café.

Falafel Mix
- 3 cups almonds, soaked overnight
- 6 Tablespoons lemon juice
- 1 Tablespoon ground cumin
- 2 Teaspoons sea salt
- ¼ cup sesame seeds, ground
- 2 Tablespoons flax, ground
- ¼ cup tahini
- ½ cup minced parsley
- ¼ Teaspoon cayenne pepper
- Additional water to thin, if needed

Spice Mix
- 2¼ cups sesame seeds, ground
- 4½ cups flax seeds, ground
- 1½ Tablespoons sea salt
- 1½ Tablespoons dried marjoram
- 1½ Tablespoons dried thyme
- 1½ Tablespoons dried oregano
- 1½ Tablespoons cumin powder

*Grind flax separately and put in a bowl. Grind sesame seeds with other herbs & salt. Store extra mix in the freezer.

Directions
1. To make falafels: Process almonds until coarsely chopped. Add lemon juice, cumin, sea salt, and cayenne to the food processor and process until combined.
2. Add the ground sesame seeds, flax seeds, tahini, and parsley and process until you have a light and fluffy mix. Test by squeezing. If they are crumbly, process again, adding ½ Tablespoon of water at a time, until it passes the squeeze test. Shape the mixture into balls – using a heaping Tablespoon.
3. To make your mix: Blend all ingredients until it becomes a powder. Put in your bowl and begin rolling each falafel in your mix, covering each falafel completely.
4. Place the falafels on mesh dehydrator sheets and dry for 10 hours, at 115°. Test at 4 hours – they should be firm on the outside and soft on the inside. It will depend on humidity – you will have to dehydrate longer on humid days.

WALNUT SAGE MEATBALLS

Makes approximately 24 meatballs

Equipment needed: Food processor, knife, cutting board, measuring cups and spoons, dehydrator

Our meatballs made their way to our pizza each day. We crumbled up the meatballs as a topping, along with veggies and sauce and our customers loved it! We also served these meatballs over our veggie pasta dishes.

Ingredients
- 4 cups of walnuts
- 3 Tablespoons nutritional yeast
- 3 Tablespoons lemon juice
- 3 Tablespoons Tamari
- 1 Tablespoon diced fresh garlic
- 1 Tablespoon onion powder
- ¼ cup, plus 1 Tablespoon, chopped fresh parsley
- 3 Tablespoons fresh chopped sage (or 2.5 Tablespoons dried)
- ½ Teaspoon sea salt

Directions
1. Process walnuts into a fine powder in your food processor.
2. Add the rest of your ingredients and process until everything is well mixed.
3. Stop the food processor as you go along and scrape down the sides of the bowl.
4. Once your mix is ready, use a Tablespoon to measure out each meatball. Roll with your hands and place on your dehydrator sheet with Teflex, at 115° for up to 10 hours.
5. You want the meatballs to still be soft on the inside, with the outside being just a little firm.
6. Keep in the refrigerator for up to two weeks in a closed glass container. You can also freeze.

TACO NUT "MEAT"

Equipment needed: Food processor, knife, cutting board, measuring cups and spoons

This "meat" was used in our taco salad entree and early on in our history of tacos. Our customers loved it so much! We would often sell it on its own, so folks could take it home and use this "meat" on their own salads and dishes.

Ingredients
- 3 cups of walnuts
- ⅓ cup soaked sun dried tomatoes
- 3 Tablespoons minced fresh parsley
- 2 Teaspoons onion powder
- 1 Teaspoon garlic powder
- 1½ Tablespoons cumin
- 2 Teaspoons chili powder
- ¼ Teaspoon cayenne pepper
- ½ Teaspoon sea salt
- 3 Tablespoons lemon juice
- 1 Tablespoon Tamari

Directions
1. Soak your walnuts the night before, in one bowl and your sun dried tomatoes in another bowl.
2. When you are ready to make your "meat", drain your walnuts and sun dried tomatoes.
3. Place your walnuts in the food processor, using the "s" blade and process until finely ground.
4. Add the rest of your ingredients and process until everything is mixed well but still has texture. You want to stop processing before it becomes a paté.
5. This "meat" will keep in your refrigerator for up to 5-7 days.

BETTER THAN TUNA PATÉ

Equipment needed: Food processor, knife, cutting board, measuring cups and spoons

This paté was used on multiple entrees over the years, as well as sold on its own in our grab n go cooler. If you're looking for a protein and fiber-rich paté with abundant flavor, this is it!

Ingredients
- 2 cups sunflower seeds
- 1 cup almonds
- ½ cup celery, minced
- ¼ cup red onion, minced
- ½ cup dulse flakes
- ¼ cup parsley, minced
- ½ cup water
- ¼ cup lemon juice
- 1 Teaspoon sea salt
- Pinch of black pepper

Directions
1. Process your sunflower seeds, almonds, water, lemon juice and sea salt in a food processor, until the nuts are ground well and then, add to a large bowl.
2. Now add your celery, red onion, parsley, dulse flakes, sea salt, pepper and lemon juice and stir well.
3. Now your paté is ready to enjoy! This will keep in your refrigerator for 5-7 days.

WALNUT PARM

Equipment needed: Food processor, measuring cups and spoons

This dairy-free take on parmesan is so easy to make and can be used in a variety of ways. It's perfect to top dishes, especially pizza and pasta.

Ingredients
- 2 cups walnuts
- ¼ cup nutritional yeast
- 1 Tablespoon sea salt
- Pinch of cayenne (optional)

Directions
1. Process all ingredients in your food processor until it forms a powder. Don't go too far or the walnuts will start to release their oil.
2. Keep in a jar in your cabinet for up to a month or in your fridge for up to six months.

DISHES

BUDDHA BOWL

The dish that started it all, our Buddha Bowl. I knew I wanted a large and filling salad on our menu that delighted the taste buds and filled the belly. I believe this salad accomplished that mission. Many of our customers told us that they couldn't eat the whole bowl in one sitting, and would often enjoy leftovers the next day. The Buddha Bowl was the epitome of abundance and vibrance on a plate.

Ingredients

- 2 cups honey spiced kale
- 2 cups salad greens
- ⅓ cup shredded carrots
- ⅓ cup shredded beets
- 1 Tablespoon fermented veggies
- 3 Herbed Falafels
- ¼ of an avocado, sliced
- Lemon Tahini Dressing – as much as you desire
- Pinch of sprouts

Directions

1. First put your kale and greens in the bowl. You can mix or have them each on half of the bowl.
2. Top with your shredded beets and carrots, then your fermented veggies, falafels and avocado.
3. Serve with as much Lemon Tahini dressing as you desire.

NACHO MAMA'S BEAN BOWL

The Nacho Mama's Bean Bowl became a huge customer favorite as soon as it landed on the menu, in our first month of business. Maybe it was the beans, maybe the Nacho Cheeze but probably the combination. I cannot tell you how many times I heard from folks who were proclaimed meat eaters who said they could not believe how filling this bowl was. And that's what I loved about Ezra's. This food is for everyone. Labels aren't needed to enjoy organic high vibration food.

Ingredients
- 2 cups salad greens
- ½ cup quinoa
- ½ cup slow cooked pinto beans
- ¼ avocado, sliced
- 1 Tablespoon fermented veggies
- 1 Teaspoon pumpkin seeds
- As much Nacho Cheeze as you desire

Directions
1. First add your greens to your bowl.
2. Now add your quinoa, beans, avocado and fermented veggies.
3. Sprinkle with pumpkin seeds and top with as much Nacho Cheeze as you desire.

ROSEMARY SWEET POTATO BOWL

I remember the day the Rosemary Sweet Potato Bowl was created. It was in our first month. We had a line out the door at the café. We had sold out of the beans and Nacho Cheeze. On the fly, I steamed some sweet potatoes, dressed them with rosemary and created a bowl with our Cashew Cheeze sauce. Our customers absolutely loved it and asked that it be on the regular menu. And thus, the Rosemary Sweet Potato Bowl was born.

Ingredients
- 2 cups salad greens
- ½ cup quinoa
- ½ cup Rosemary Sweet Potatoes
- ¼ avocado, sliced
- 1 Tablespoon fermented veggies
- 1 Teaspoon pumpkin seeds
- As much Cashew Cheeze sauce as you desire

Directions
1. First add your greens to your bowl.
2. Now add your quinoa, sweet potato, avocado and fermented veggies.
3. Sprinkle with pumpkin seeds and top with as much Cashew Cheeze as you desire.

SIMPLE TRUTH BOWL

We created the Simple Truth Bowl to give our customers a lunch option that was more affordable and still deeply nourishing. Just a bit more simple. And thus, the bowl and the name were born.

Ingredients
- ¾ cup cooked rice
- ⅓ cup slow cooked pinto beans
- ¼ cup honey spiced kale

Directions
1. Add your greens first, then your beans and lastly your rice.
2. Feel free to top with anything you like, such as fermented veggies or Lemon Tahini Dressing.

OPEN-FACED BAGEL

Our customers who were gluten-free really loved this dish. To have a gluten-free house-made bagel, without preservatives and fillers, is uncommon. You can now make your own with the Everything Almond Flax Bagel recipe in this book. This recipe is just one way to make yourself a meal with the bagel. Our customers loved this flavorful menu offering.

Ingredients
- Half of your Everything Almond Flax Bagel, toasted
- 2 Tablespoons Cashew Cheeze Sauce
- 4 thin slices of cucumber
- ¼ avocado, sliced
- 1 Tablespoon red onion, diced
- 1 Tablespoon Curry Dressing
- 1 Teaspoon hemp seeds
- Pinch of fresh sprouts

Directions
1. Spread your Cashew Cheeze Sauce on your bagel.
2. Layer your slices of cucumber, then your avocado, and then a sprinkle of red onion.
3. Drizzle over your Curry Dressing, then sprinkle your hemp seeds, and top with your sprouts.

SWEET POTATO QUINOA BURGER WRAPS

Equipment needed: Knife, tablespoon, cutting board

These wraps found themselves with almost a cult following. We would stock our grab n go in the morning, and often they would be gone by the end of the lunch rush. Our customers loved them because they were so easy to grab and eat in the car, or at work or anywhere. This wrap is incredibly filling, flavorful and does not weigh you down.

Ingredients
- 1 Sweet Potato Quinoa Burger, cut in half
- 1 large collard leaf, stem removed
- 2 Tablespoons Quinoa Burger Sauce
- ¼ avocado, thinly sliced
- 1 slice of tomato, cut in half
- 6 thin slices of red onion
- A pinch of sprouts

Directions
1. The first thing you want to do is to have both sides of the collard leaf layed out and ready to wrap. Cut out the stem, so you have two sides of your collard leaf.
2. Spread 1 Tablespoon of your Quinoa Burger Sauce in the middle of each leaf.
3. Now, on each leaf, place a half of your burger on top of the sauce.
4. Next, layer on your avocado, tomato, slices of red onion and pinch of sprouts.
5. Lastly, you can roll each up until you have two small wraps.

CHAPTER

9

DESSERT

Ahh, desserts. By the time we closed our doors, our desserts were the number one seller at our café. In fact, when we first opened, I pictured Ezra's Café being more of a wellness juice bar that served chocolates and desserts. I laugh at that now, looking at what we quickly grew into serving. But our desserts remained a staple. Our customers remember that shiny dessert case that greeted them when they walked in, offering 30 or so desserts at a time.

As with all of our menu, over the years, our dessert selection grew as we became inspired as a team and created new, fun treats. In this recipe book, we are offering you recipes that we have hand selected from our collection.

Over the years, many customers told us how special it was to be able to enjoy a cheesecake or brownie and it would be safe for them to eat. We had mothers and grandmothers bringing in children with gluten and dairy sensitivities. Dessert makes people happy to stop time for a moment and simply enjoy life. This is such an important part of being human. Being able to treat ourselves and slow down for a moment of pure pleasure, is a joyful part of life. We showed our community just how amazing dessert can be, even without dairy and gluten. We never used soy or tofu. Only whole and unprocessed organic and NON-GMO ingredients.

A few things to note:

When making your cakes, I recommend putting either plastic wrap or parchment paper at the bottom of your cake pan. It makes it easier to release the cake from the pan. You can place your pan over your parchment paper and draw a circle then cut, to give you the perfect size.

There is something we called "the squeeze test" when making crusts or cookies. You want your cake crusts and cookies to be able to stay together and not just crumble. Being that our desserts are completely raw and not cooked, you do not have the baking process to bring everything together like a conventional dessert. When making your crust in your food processor, you want to take a little bit and squeeze in your hand. If you squeeze the crust and it still crumbles, or doesn't stick together well, you can add a tiny bit of water - sometimes even a ½ of a teaspoon, and then process again and squeeze. If it still crumbles, add a bit more water and squeeze again. Once the crust (or cookie) stays in place when you squeeze, it's ready. Be mindful not to overprocess until you have a blob. It should only stick together when you press down or squeeze.

CHOCOLATE SAUCE

Equipment needed: Blender and measuring cups

I think it is safe to say that our kitchen at Ezra's was never without this Chocolate Sauce. We used it in so many items, including desserts, but also a number of our smoothies and herbal tonics. We liked to keep it in squeeze bottles, which made it very easy to use. I do recommend investing in a kitchen squeeze bottle if you plan to use this sauce to make designs on your cakes or in your smoothies.

Ingredients
- ¾ cup maple syrup
- ¾ cup cacao powder
- ⅓ cup coconut oil (does not need to be melted beforehand)
- 1 pinch sea salt

Directions
1. Blend all ingredients until smooth.
2. Keep in the refrigerator for up to 6 months.
3. This Chocolate Sauce is safe to leave on the counter for a day or two, if you are using it frequently, but it will last longer in the fridge. You will also want to gently warm your sauce before using it when you take it out of your refrigerator. You can do this by placing the bottle or container into a bowl of warm to hot water for a few minutes.

LIVING KEYLIME CHEEZECAKE

Yields 16 slices

Equipment needed: Food processor, blender, knife, springform pan, measuring spoons and cups, spatula, cutting board

Our Keylime Cheezecake was on the menu from day one at the café. She remained one of our most popular desserts until our last day open. In 2016, we were actually on the show Good Eats on the Cooking Channel, showcasing this delicious dessert. This cake is the perfect combination of sweet and tart. The cake is creamy and the crust is satisfyingly soft and a little crumbly.

Crust ingredients
- 2 cups organic raw almonds
- 3 Tablespoons coconut flakes
- ½ cup pitted and chopped dates
- 2 Tablespoons maple syrup
- ½ Teaspoon sea salt

Filling ingredients
- 1 cup fresh squeezed lime juice
- 2 cups cashews
- 1 cup macadamia nuts
- ½ cup maple syrup
- ½ cup coconut oil, gently melted
- ¼ cup almond mylk
- ¼ Teaspoon vanilla extract

Directions
1. To make your crust: Process your almonds and sea salt until coarsely chopped. Add coconut flakes and pulse. Add your dates to your food processor and process until you have a fine meal.
2. Stream in your maple syrup as you pulse once more.
3. Use the squeeze test to ensure your crust will not flake when you cut it.
4. Fill your springform pan with your crust and press down evenly.
5. To make your filling: Blend everything but coconut oil until smooth. Stream in coconut oil until completely smooth and combined.
6. Pour the filling over your crust and smooth out with a spatula. Sprinkle with fresh lime coconut topping.
7. Cover with plastic wrap or foil, and freeze for 3 hours or even overnight, until completely set and firm.
8. To serve: Pull your cake out of the freezer and let it sit for 30 minutes to an hour, depending on how warm it is in your kitchen. Use a knife to score the top into 16 even pieces. Then run your knife under hot water, dry and carefully cut a slice. Serve or put back into your freezer until ready to serve.

CHOCOLATE MOCHA BLISS CAKE

Yields 16 slices

Equipment needed: Food processor, blender, knife, 8-inch springform pan, measuring spoons and cups, cutting board

Chocolate, coffee and cake. For some, this is heaven. We created this cake to delight the hard core chocolate lovers and it was a favorite until the last day we were open.

Crust ingredients
- 2 cups walnuts
- 1 Teaspoon sea salt
- ½ cup cacao powder
- 1 Tablespoon coconut sugar
- 1 Tablespoon Dandy Blend
- 1½ cup pitted and chopped dates

Sauce for the middle layer ingredients
- 2¾ cups maple syrup
- 2¾ cups cacao powder
- 1⅓ cups coconut oil
- 3 pinches of salt

Filling ingredients
- 3½ cups cashews
- ¾ cup almond mylk
- ⅓ cup fresh coffee, chilled
- ½ cup almond butter
- 2 Tablespoons Dandy Blend
- ¼ cup cacao powder
- ½ cup plus 2 Tablespoons maple syrup
- ¼ Teaspoon vanilla
- ⅓ cup melted cacao butter
- 3 pinches of sea salt

Directions
1. To make your crust: Process all except the dates into a dust. Add your dates and process again until you have a crust. Then press into your cake pan.
2. Pour 1 ½ cups Chocolate Sauce over the crust and freeze for 20 minutes.
3. Take your crust out of the freezer. Sprinkle 2 Tablespoons cacao nibs over the Chocolate Sauce.
4. To make filling: Blend all ingredients until smooth and creamy. Then pour the filling into the cake pan.
5. Put your cake back into the freezer for at least 1 hour to set. Take it back out of the freezer and pour 1 cup Chocolate Sauce over the top. Sprinkle with 2 more Tablespoons cacao nibs. Freeze for another hour and it will be ready to cut and serve.
6. Best way to cut your cake: Use a knife to score the top into 16 even pieces. Then run the knife under hot water, dry and carefully cut a slice. Serve, or put it back into the freezer until ready to serve.

MINT CHOCOLATE CHEEZECAKE

Yields 16 slices

Equipment needed: Food processor, blender, knife, springform pan, measuring spoons and cups, cutting board

This cake was a special item that came out around Valentine's Day and Mothers Day every year. That classic combination of chocolate and mint, with the creamy filling and satisfyingly rich crust…oooh baby this one is good!

Crust ingredients
- 2 cups of almonds
- ½ cup coconut flour
- 1 Teaspoon sea salt
- ¼ cup cacao powder
- 1 cup date paste
- Chocolate Sauce – about 1 cup

Sprinkles for 2nd layer over chocolate ingredients
- ¼ cup cacao nibs
- ¼ cup coconut sugar

Filling ingredients
- 3 cups of cashews
- 4½ Tablespoons coconut butter
- ¼ cup cacao butter, melted
- ½ Teaspoon vanilla
- 1 Tablespoon E3Live Renew Me powder
- 1 Tablespoon peppermint extract (taste for flavor)
- 1 cup almond mylk
- ½ cup maple syrup
- ¼ Teaspoon sea salt

Directions
1. To make the date paste: Blend 1 cup of dates with ⅓ cup water until smooth.
2. To make your crust: Process almonds first, until they are a fine powder. Add coconut flour, salt and cacao powder and process quickly, until combined. Add your date paste and process again until your dough forms. MAKE SURE YOU DON'T OVER PROCESS.
3. Make sure you have your Chocolate Sauce made in advance.
4. To make your filling: Blend all ingredients in your blender until smooth and creamy.
5. Okay, now let's assemble the cake! Press your crust into the bottom of your pan evenly.
6. Pour 1 cup of your Chocolate Sauce over the crust and smooth out evenly. Save the rest of the sauce in the fridge.
7. Sprinkle your second layer evenly (cacao nib/coconut sugar mix).
8. Pour your filling evenly over the nibs and sugar. Gently tap your cake pan on your counter to dispel any bubbles and ensure everything is evenly layered.
9. To decorate: Make any design you like on top of your cake with Chocolate Sauce and use a toothpick to swirl. You can also wait to decorate until the cake is set in the freezer.
10. Now freeze for 4 hours or overnight, to set.
11. To Serve: Slice into 16 pieces and serve with Chocolate Sauce, mint leaves and cacao.
12. Best way to cut your cake: Use a knife to score the top into 16 even pieces. Then run the knife under hot water, dry and carefully cut a slice. Serve or put back into the freezer until ready to serve.

PUMPKIN CHOCOLATE CHEEZECAKE

Yields 16 slices

Equipment needed: Food processor, blender, knife, springform pan, measuring spoons and cups, cutting board

The Pumpkin Chocolate Cheezecake made her appearance right around Thanksgiving every year at the café and was a limited time cake. Once the holidays were over, it was another year before she was available. Our customers would often purchase multiple slices to keep in their freezer because she's just that good!

Crust ingredients
- 2½ cups walnuts
- 1 cup dates
- 2 pinches sea salt
- 1 Tablespoon maple syrup

Chocolate Filling ingredients
- ¾ cup maple syrup
- ¾ cup cacao powder
- ⅓ cup coconut oil (does not need to be melted beforehand)
- 1 pinch of sea salt

Pumpkin filling ingredients
- 3 cups RAW sweet potatoes, chopped
- 3 cups cashews
- 2 Tablespoons pumpkin pie spice
- ¾ cup maple syrup
- ½ cup coconut oil
- ½ cup water

Directions
1. To make your crust: Process walnuts with salt, until ground, in the food processor.
2. Add dates and process until the crust begins to stick together.
3. Stream in maple syrup while processing.
4. Transfer crust to your 9-inch round springform pan. Press firmly and evenly on the bottom of the pan.
5. Now you will make your Chocolate Sauce and pour 1 cup over the crust. Put into the freezer to set, while you are making the filling.
6. To make your filling: Chop your raw sweet potatoes into diced cubes. Blend sweet potatoes in your blender until creamy (use a wand to push down potatoes while blending). Add a little of the ½ cup of water at a time, but don't add more than ½ cup water all together. Add the rest of the ingredients and blend until smooth.
7. Pour filling into your springform pan. Put into the freezer to set for 4 hours or overnight.
8. Now you can decorate with extra Chocolate Sauce if you desire before serving.

LIVING LEMON SQUARES

Yields 9 squares

Equipment needed: Food processor, blender, micro-plane, measuring spoons and cups, knife, spatula, 8x8 tart pan

Lemons are full of antioxidants – anti-aging and cleansing to the body. How amazing is it that we can have a delicious dessert that also supports our well-being?! These Lemon Squares were served up every day for the 7 ½ years we were open. A much loved treat. Creamy, tart and sweet!

Bar ingredients
- 3 cups almonds
- 1¼ cups dates, pitted and chopped
- ½ Teaspoon salt
- zest from three lemons
- ¼ Teaspoon vanilla extract
- 2½ Tablespoons of fresh lemon juice
- ⅔ cup coconut flakes

Frosting ingredients
- 1 cup cashews, soaked
- 3½ Tablespoons lemon juice (zest lemons first and save for topping)
- 1 Tablespoon coconut oil
- 1 Teaspoon honey
- ⅛ Teaspoon vanilla extract
- 3 Tablespoons water

Topping ingredients
- ⅓ cup coconut flakes
- 2 Tablespoons lemon zest

Directions
1. To make bars: Process almonds in your food processor until you have a fine powder. Add salt, dates, zest, vanilla, and lemon juice, and process until you have flaky "dough" that sticks together when you pinch it. Put your mixture into a large bowl and add coconut flakes, mixing in with your hands. Press your dough into your square tart pan and set aside.
2. To make frosting: First, you'll want to soak your cashews in water for an hour then rinse. Blend all ingredients in a blender until smooth and creamy – using a spatula to help push the mixture back down as it migrates up the sides of the blender.
3. Spread your frosting over your bars evenly.
4. Combine zest and coconut flakes in a small bowl, then sprinkle over the top.
5. Refrigerate for 1 hour before serving.
6. Good to serve for 3-4 days if refrigerated. You can also freeze and serve as desired.

TRIPLE CHOCOLATE BROWNIES

Yields 12 brownie squares

Equipment needed: Food processor, blender, Vita-Mix, spatula, fluted 13.75 x 4.25 inch tart pan, measuring cups and spoons, cutting board

Another original recipe that stood the test of time at Ezra's. This was our no frills brownie – simply chocolate through and through and an absolute beloved treat by so many of our customers.

Crust ingredients
- 3 cups walnuts
- ⅔ cup dates, pitted and chopped
- ½ cup cacao
- ⅓ Teaspoon salt
- ½ Tablespoon of water, IF NEEDED, to make crust stick together Use the squeeze test!
- Chocolate Sauce – about 1 cup pre-made for this recipe

Directions
1. To make your crust: In a food processor, process walnuts with the S-blade until powdered. Add dates and process again, until well combined.
2. Add cacao powder, salt, and process until everything is mixed thoroughly. **Do not over blend or your mixture will become oily.
3. Place brownie crust into a long rectangular silver pan.
4. Pour Chocolate Sauce slowly, starting from the center. Stop pouring, then tilt the pan from side to side distributing evenly. Use a cake frosting spatula to spread the rest of the Chocolate Sauce evenly. Sprinkle with cacao nibs.
5. Place in the freezer to firm for 2 hours. Once firm, cut into the sizes of your choice.

SALTED ALMOND CHOCOLATE FUDGE

Yields 20 squares

Equipment needed: Blender, spatula, fluted 13.75 x 4.25 inch tart pan, measuring cups and spoons, cutting board

If you're looking for something super rich and you love the combination of almond butter and chocolate, this could be the dessert for you.

Fudge ingredients
- 2½ cups smooth organic almond butter
- ½ cup organic coconut oil
- ¾ cup cacao butter, melted
- ½ cup pure maple syrup
- ½ Teaspoon sea salt
- Chocolate Sauce – you'll need about 1 cup pre-made

Directions
1. Lightly oil your tart pan and line with a piece of parchment paper, cut to fit the length of the pan.
2. For the fudge: In a small pot, add the coconut oil, maple syrup, cacao butter and salt. Heat over low, until the oil is melted. Slowly pour the wet mixture into a small bowl with the almond butter, stirring as you go. Stir until completely smooth and combined.
3. With a spatula, spoon the fudge mixture into the prepared pan and smooth it out. Place the pan, uncovered, on a flat surface in the freezer. Freeze for at least an hour, until the fudge is firm all the way through.
4. For the chocolate topping: Make sure you have about 1 cup of the Chocolate Sauce pre-made.
5. To serve: Take your fudge from the freezer and let sit for 5-10 minutes so it won't break when cutting. Score the fudge into squares the size of your choice. Cut them into squares. Cover the top of each square with just enough Chocolate Sauce to cover it. You can serve as is or set the fudge in the refrigerator to harden the Chocolate Sauce a bit before serving.

CHOCOLATE CHIP COOKIES

Yields 15 1 oz cookies

Equipment needed: Food processor, blender, dehydrator with white mesh tray, measuring cups and spoons, knife, cutting board

These cookies are bite size and perfect to satisfy that sweet tooth, without having a large portion. Keep them frozen or warm them up before you enjoy them…either way they are a truly chocolaty, delicious treat.

Cookie ingredients
- 1 cup oats, ground into powder
- ½ cup dates, pitted and chopped
- 1 cup walnuts, ground into powder
- 2 Tablespoons almond butter
- ½ Teaspoon sea salt
- ¼ Teaspoon vanilla extract
- ¼ cup cacao nibs
- ½ cup Chocolate Sauce

Directions
1. Add all ingredients, except cacao nibs, into your food processor and process until dough forms. **Do not over process as over processed nuts become oily. Put dough into a large bowl and fold in cacao nibs.
2. Roll your dough into balls, place on your dehydrator mesh sheet and press down, creating a cookie shape – do not over flatten – it should be a thicker cookie. Press down in the center to leave a little space for your Chocolate Sauce to sit.
3. Dehydrate at 135° for 1 hour. Turn down to 115° and dehydrate for another hour.
4. Top each cookie with your Chocolate Sauce (approximately 1 Teaspoon) and place the cookies in the freezer to set for 30 minutes.
5. Each cookie should weigh approximately 1 oz. before chocolate sauce is put on.

CHOCOLATE COCONUT MACAROONS

Yields 50 macaroons

Equipment needed: Large bowl, dehydrator, measuring cups and spoons

I remember having chocolate macaroons while traveling years before we opened the café and I loved them so much I did my best to recreate them myself. These macaroons were the result and remained a staple in our dessert case; bite size, deep, rich, chocolaty goodness.

Ingredients
- 3 cups dried coconut flakes
- 1½ cups cacao powder
- 1 cup maple syrup
- ⅓ cup coconut oil, melted
- 1 Tablespoon vanilla
- ½ Teaspoon sea salt

Directions
1. To make your happy, healthy macaroons: Mix all ingredients together in a large bowl until completely mixed, making sure there is no dried powder left.
2. Roll into balls, using approximately 1 Tablespoon per macaroon.
3. Dehydrate at 110 for 3 hours.
4. Put in the freezer to cool for 1 hour before enjoying. They keep beautifully in the freezer for months.

CHOCOLATE AVOCADO MOUSSE

Equipment needed: Food processor, measuring cups and spoons, spatula

There are some of us who truly love the creamy soft feel of a chocolate mousse. The beauty of this version is that it's made with fresh avocados. Truly full of fiber and so rich and creamy. Like eating a chocolate cloud!

Ingredients
- ½ cup pitted dates, soaked in water for 2 hours, then drained
- ½ cup maple syrup
- 1 Teaspoon vanilla extract
- 1½ cups mashed avocado (about 3 avocados)
- ½ cup cacao powder
- ¼ cup carob powder
- 1 Teaspoon raw mesquite powder
- 1 Teaspoon cinnamon
- ½ cup water

Directions
1. Process dates, maple syrup, and vanilla in a food processor until smooth.
2. Add in the rest of the ingredients and process until creamy.
3. Stop and scrape down the sides of the processor bowl with a spatula as needed. Gradually add the water and process until smooth.
4. Serve with love!

DONUTS

Yields approximately 10 donuts

Equipment needed: Food processor, blender, bowls, tongs, plate or tray, measuring cups and spoons

Our donuts became an absolute hit once we added them to the menu and before we knew it, we had three different flavor options.

Donut Ingredients
- 1 cup soaked and rinsed almonds (2/3 cup dry)
- ⅔ cup oats
- ⅔ cup of dates
- ¼ Teaspoon sea salt

Glaze Ingredients
- ¾ cup of maple syrup
- 1 cup of coconut oil
- ¼ Teaspoon vanilla

Cinnamon Ingredients
- ¼ cup coconut sugar
- ¼ cup cinnamon

Chocolate Sauce Ingredients
- ¾ cup maple syrup
- ¾ cup cacao powder
- ⅓ cup coconut oil (does not need to be melted beforehand)
- 1 pinch sea salt

Directions
1. To make your donuts: Process all ingredients until dough forms. Use the squeeze test. If your donut mix isn't sticking together well or is a bit crumbly, you can add a teaspoon of water at a time and process until it passes the squeeze test. Shape into 1.5 oz balls, then press down gently to make a disk. You can use the end of a wooden handle or a chopstick to gently make a hole in the center. Now add to your freezer to firm.
2. For Glazed donuts: Blend your glaze ingredients until smooth and add to a bowl. Use tongs to hold your donut and dip into the glaze. Place your donuts on a tray or plate and put back into the freezer until your glaze hardens.
3. For Cinnamon donuts: Dip glazed donuts in cinnamon mix before putting into the freezer.
4. For Chocolate donuts: Blend your chocolate sauce ingredients and add sauce to a bowl. Dip your donuts in the chocolate using tongs, then place on a tray or plate and add to the freezer to set and firm.
5. Serve with love!

CARROT SPICE MUFFINS

Yields 6 muffins

Equipment needed: Food processor, bowls, measuring cups and spoons, muffin molds, dehydrator

The Carrot Spice Muffins were created just for the café before we opened our doors, and stayed a customer favorite until our last day. This muffin is incredibly dense and filling. Perhaps a breakfast on the go or a midday snack. We also use this muffin in two of our bowls, which recipes are included in this book.

Ingredients
- 3 cups rolled oats, ground in your food processor
- ¾ cup soaked & rinsed walnuts
- ¼ cup soaked & rinsed pecans
- 1 cup shredded carrot
- ¼ cup shredded coconut
- ¼ cup water
- 1 Tablespoon pumpkin pie spice
- ½ Tablespoon cinnamon
- ¼ cup raisins
- ¼ Teaspoon salt
- ⅓ cup maple syrup

Additional ingredients, after the first process of the dough:
- ¾ cup shredded carrots
- ⅓ cup raisins

Directions
1. Soak walnuts and pecans overnight and then rinse.
2. Process all ingredients in your food processor until the batter mixes together.
3. Add in ½ cup more shredded carrot and ⅓ cup more raisins and process so batter is still chunky with carrots and raisins.
4. Scoop out your batter (about 6 ½ oz per muffin) and fill approximately 6 muffin/cupcake silicone molds. Dehydrate for 1 hour at 115°. Take muffins out of molds and dehydrate for 2-3 hours more.

CASHEW YOGURT BERRY PARFAIT

Equipment needed: Bowl, blender, knife, cutting board, spatula

These parfaits came on the scene very early in the cafe's history. They became so popular in our final years, we often sold out before lunch and then would make a second batch. You can pre-make your yogurt, parfait and granola so that you have the ingredients to quickly make yourself a parfait in the morning. You can also pre-make them to just grab on your way to work or play.

Cashew Yogurt Ingredients
- 3 cups cashews
- 4 Tablespoons maple syrup
- ½ Teaspoon lemon juice
- ½ Teaspoon coconut oil
- 1¼ cups coconut mylk
- ⅛ Teaspoon sea salt
- Dash of vanilla extract

To make your yogurt:
1. Add all of your ingredients in the blender and blend until smooth.
2. Add more mylk, if needed for the yogurt to be pourable. You want it to be smooth and glossy and easily pourable. It will set up and thicken in the fridge a bit as well.

Berry Puree Ingredients
- 2 cups of strawberries
- 2 cups of frozen blueberries, thawed
- 1 Teaspoon lemon juice
- ½ Teaspoon maple syrup

To make your berry puree:
1. Add all of your ingredients into your blender and blend until smooth.
2. Using frozen blueberries will make the berry flavor and color deeper.

To make your parfait, in your favorite parfait dish or cup:
1. Add a layer of your Buckwheat Lime Granola.
2. Next add a layer of your cashew yogurt.
3. Next add fresh sliced strawberries.
4. Now add a layer of your puree.
5. Repeat as desired and enjoy!

MEDICINE BALLS

Yields approximately 29 Medicine Balls

Equipment needed: Large bowl, spatula or spoon, measuring cups and spoons

We created this dessert to be a vehicle for deep medicine in a sweet delicious treat. It became one of our most popular desserts for years. Enjoy!

Ingredients
- 2 cups tahini
- 1 cup raw local honey
- ¼ cup cacao powder
- 2 Tablespoons hemp seeds
- 2 Tablespoons Dandy Blend
- 1 Tablespoon astragalus powder

- 1 Tablespoon reishi mushroom
- 1 Tablespoon chaga mushroom
- ½ Teaspoon cinnamon
- Sprinkle of sea salt
- 1 cup shredded coconut
- ½ cup pumpkin seeds

Superfood dust
- ¼ cup hemp seeds
- ½ cup bee local pollen

Directions

1. In a large mixing bowl, combine your tahini and honey until smooth.
2. Add in all other ingredients, except the shredded coconut and pumpkin seeds, and mix until combined.
3. The consistency should be thick enough to make into balls but not dry enough to feel the powdered herbs. So don't be afraid to add more powders or nut butter to get the consistency you want. Remember, we are working with living food, so hydration and consistency of ingredients can change each time you make this recipe.
4. Roll into 2 Tablespoon-sized balls then roll in your superfood dust mix so each ball is well coated.
5. Add to the freezer for an hour to set. Keep refrigerated and enjoy anytime you need a boost to your energy or your immune system or both!

KNOWLEDGE IS POWER

Ezra's Enlightened Cafe

When we learn and understand our outer environment, we are better able to find our way in the world. Our well-being. Our happiness. I have always believed this.

When I learned just how powerful the right foods and herbs can be in overall health and quality of life, I wanted to share it with the world. I taught classes every single month at Ezra's Cafe'. Many of those classes sold out and we had folks packed in our tiny space, ready to learn something new and to be inspired.

These classes hold some of my most precious memories of Ezra's Cafe'. There is something so special about humans gathering together, in person, with a goal or thing in common. For just that blip of time, an experience is shared by just those people. If you attended our classes, thank you for being part of those experiences.

I hope this book provides nourishment for your body and soul. If you were a customer of the café, I hope these recipes bring you the joy of not only the food but the memories.

Always keep learning. Stretch your mind with new ideas. And listen to your body. It will never lie to you.

And so it is done. Blessed Be.
Audrey

CITATIONS

https://pubmed.ncbi.nlm.nih.gov/31447137/

https://pubmed.ncbi.nlm.nih.gov/32096470/

https://foodrevolution.org/blog/what-is-miso/

https://pubmed.ncbi.nlm.nih.gov/18989835/

https://www.greenamerica.org/blog/gmo-timeline-history-genetically-modified-foods

https://www.nongmoproject.org/gmo-facts/what-is-gmo/

AUTHOR BIOGRAPHY

Audrey Barron lives with her husband Sam and two children, Ezra and Elliana, in Indianapolis. She is the retired Owner of Ezra's Café. Now a fullt-time Herbalist and Urban farmer at Wild Moon Acres, Audrey can be found growing herbs, making medicines and teaching workshops. You can find Audrey at www.gaiachef.com and learn about the farm at www. wildmoonacres.love

Printed in the United States
by Baker & Taylor Publisher Services